Retail Banking

*

Dr. Ramamurthy N
M.Sc., B.G.L., C.A.I.I.B., C.C.P., D.S.A.D.P., C.I.S.A., P.M.P., CGBL, Ph.D.

*

2013

Name of the Book: **Retail Banking**

First Edition: 2013

Author: **Dr. Ramamurthy N**
                    http://ramamurthy.jaagruti.co.in/

Copyright ©:   With the author (No part of this book may be
                    reproduced in any manner whatsoever without
                    the written permission from the author).

ISBN(13):   978-81-910336-7-0

ISBN 978-81-910336-7-0

9 788191 033670 >

Number of Pages: 211

*****

TABLE OF CONTENTS

*****

Dedication

I dedicate this book to the entire Banking Industry of the globe which brought me to this level.

Dr. Ramamurthy N

*****

Foreword

It is needless to mention that clear understanding of the key banking functions is *sine qua non* of success in contemporary sophisticated banking. By bringing together the major terms associated with Retail Banking, this book aims to provide readers with a single and easily accessible source of generally accepted retail banking functions and practices.

As the author has clearly mentioned, the perceptions and dimensions of banking have drastically changed in recent times. Most of the banking operations are automated. Some banks also use outsourced agencies for most of the banking needs like Account Opening, Loan Origination, etc. This makes it all the more important that the customers should be aware of the banking operations/ processes.

Mr. Ramamurthy has meticulously included recent banking topics like Financial Inclusion, Islamic Banking, etc. This will definitely elicit interest among the readers on this economically efficient and widely acclaimed type of banking. Most of these concepts are very new to the common public and probably for some bankers even. I could perceive not only theory but practical experience in the coverage of the book. Definitely this will be useful for the students as well.

Mr. **Ramamurthy** has diversified experience in different walks of banking – varied dimensions like manual banking, automated banking and offering IT solutions to global banks. Having acquired this much varied qualifications, experience and expertise, he also has chosen to spread his knowledge through conducting training programs, speaking at seminars and now penning different books.

With over three decades of domain experience in Banking and Information Technology, he has been a consultant to a few Foreign Banks, Companies, Universities and Spiritual Associations. With fire in his belly for continuous self-development, he is pursuing his Doctoral Dissertation titled "IT in Samskrit" with University of Madras. As part of his consultancy assignments, he has crisscrossed the globe and met a large number of professionals during which interactions he rightly felt the need for authoring such a book. He has kneaded his years of practical experience and has used the principle of applied terminology in this book, which will advance the knowledge of arcane field of Retail Banking.

Mr. Ramamurthy has authored books on as diverse subjects as Finance, IT and Spiritualism. My best wishes to him for coming out with more such books.

With treasures inside, this book is a confidence building addition for people both with and without experience in retail banking. At a time of increased thrust on retail banking, Mr Ramamurthy's book has come not a day too soon. I am sure the readers will immensely benefit from his rich experience he has brought to bear on this book.

Chennai   *Srinivas Acharya*
13th February 2012   **Managing Director**
                            Sundaram BNP Paribas Home Finance

*****

Preface

Earlier the banking industry was service oriented – they had different counters for Savings, Term Deposit, Current Account, etc. But after the advent of Core Banking System, thanks to Western Banking, it all has become product oriented – Retail, Corporate, etc. The banks do not have clients for their services, but have customers, instead, for their products. The facet of the entire banking industry across the globe is undergoing a complete manifestation.

The author has experienced three different perspectives about banking as:

- Manual Banking process
- Using automated banking process
- Offering IT solutions to automate banking processes across the globe

Various trainees, who attended the author's various training programmes under banking, requested him to write a general book about **Retail Banking**. This book is aimed at the audience of non-bankers. This does not go deep into the micro level operations of the bank. But, on the other hand, explains the concepts of banking to the common man – probably the customers of banks.

At a higher plane, banks offer their retail customers portfolio management services. When retail banking transcends beyond a level, it metamorphoses into private banking. In simple terms it can be understood that Retail Banking deal with individual customers and Corporate Banking deals with business entities.

While this book primarily deals with Retail Banking areas viz., Deposits, Retail Lending, Cards, Other Services of a Bank, etc., the latest trends in Banking like Financial Inclusion, Islamic Banking, Channel of Banking, Banking Landscape, Analysis of Bank Balance Sheet, etc., are also discussed. Separate book on **Corporate Banking** has been written by the same author, which covers Working Capital analysis, Appraisal of Corporate Loans, etc.

There is subtle difference in Banking Theory, Law and Practice. Those are also noted in this book wherever possible. As pointed out earlier banking has become product oriented, which brings the concept of marketing in banks. Hence a chapter on Bank Marketing is also added. Currently the banking is no more account related – it is all about marketing, relationship and a kind of computer operation. Hence a chapter on Bank Marketing is more apt and relevant in the current trend.

This book mainly talks about Indian banking system, of course, the root of which is British system. However, with the world-wide experience of the author, almost all the areas are compared with global banking scenarios. To make the book update on the recent developments in banking system, a chapter on AML is also included.

The author came across an anonymous material (basically a copy of a computer printout) without the name of the author or source, etc. This material did give quiet some inputs into deposits, payment system and card areas included in this book. The unknown author of this material is duly acknowledged.

A sincere thanks to Mr. Srinivas Acharya, who has written a foreword for this book and a couple of pleasantries about the author.

Definitely my sincere thanks are due are due to Mr. Pradeep Mittal of LPP Publications for bringing up this book in the form it is in the hands of the readers. Nice job done Mr. Pradeep.

The readers can feel free to contact the author for any comments/feedback.

Chennai
November 2013   Dr. *Ramamurthy N*

*****

Chapter 1.   Financial System

As all of us are aware, banks do not exist in a vacuum. They are an important and at the same time an integral part of the very financial system. Hence, to understand banks and banking, it is desirable to get a macro perspective of the financial system as a whole.

This leads us to the fundamental question as to what constitutes the financial system. It is a set (or aggregation) of institutions, instruments, markets and services. A complex interplay of these components makes the financial system vibrant. As with any other system, the financial system too has an overriding objective, i.e. to ensure smooth flow of money from those who have surplus to those who has demand, so that the latter can make an effective use of the same, benefiting in the process themselves and the economy as a whole.

1.1. Financial System - Constituents

Financial Services can be broadly defined as follows:

- A term used to describe organisations that deal with the management of money
- Provide a variety of money and investment and related services
- Banks, investment banks, insurance companies, credit card companies and stock brokerages, Credit unions, Non-Banking Financial Institutions - all of them together make the financial system.
- It is the largest industry (or industry category) in the world, in terms of earnings
- On the average, the industry represents 20% of the market capitalisation

1.2. Financial Institutions

As the very name makes it obvious, these institutions are, engaged in the business of 'finance'. They can further be decomposed into three sub-categories:

- Intermediaries
- Non-Intermediaries
- Regulatory Agencies

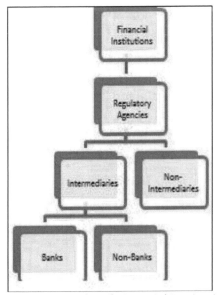

Figure 1 – Hierarchy of Financial Institutions

Intermediaries: As is obvious from the very name, intermediaries are those financial institutions that accept deposit and channelise the same as lending/ investment. In other words, financial intermediaries function as a bridge between those who has surplus money and those who has demand in any economy. Take away these intermediaries. The financial system as well as the entire economy would more or less come to a standstill. In fact, financial intermediaries by their smooth "conduit function" make the economy infinitely more efficient in the usage of money. Examples of financial intermediaries are: Banks, Non -Banking Finance Companies (NBFCs), Insurance Companies, Mutual Funds, etc.

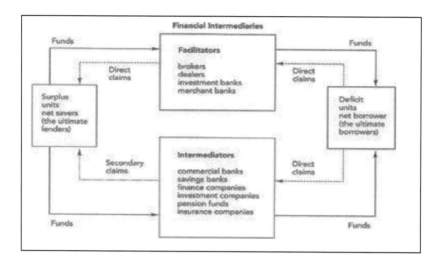

Non-intermediaries: Besides intermediaries, there are also financial institutions which function as non-intermediaries. These institutions fund the users of money, but do not, as a matter of policy, accept deposits from ordinary public. Classic examples of such institutions can be broking agencies, fund managers, etc. In the Indian context, a good number of State Financial Corporations could have been classified as non-intermediaries. For Instance, in Tamil Nadu, institutions such as SIDCO and TIIC started as pure non-intermediaries. But the billion dollar question could be, if these institutions were/ are funding borrowers, where from they were/ are getting their funds? Not from depositors, but from their owners or members as capital contribution/ subscription.

Regulatory agencies: The financial institutional turf does not get complete with just intermediaries and non-intermediaries. In addition, there are agencies whose sole function is to monitor and regulate the functioning of such intermediaries and non-intermediaries. These are in short called "regulatory agencies". They are like the traffic cops. They lay down the "Do's and Don'ts" for the other players in the market. To make their regulations enforceable, these agencies are generally armed with punitive powers, which can be exercised in case of non-compliance by any of the players. Central Bank of any country (Reserve Bank of India, Federal

Reserve, etc.), for instance, is the regulatory agency *vis-à-vis* the banking system. Similarly, Securities and Exchange Board of India is responsible for regulating the capital market segment. Insurance Regulatory bodies are responsible for controlling insurance (both life and non-life).

1.3. Financial Markets

As one of the components of the financial system, financial markets represent the real/ virtual markets where financial instruments get traded. Thus, one has share market where shares, bonds and other securities bonds issued by different corporates get traded. Similarly, Government Securities market is for buying and selling securities issued by the sovereign. There is yet another market, namely, money market where very liquid instruments such as Treasury Bills, short term Government papers, etc., - get traded. Forex market is where one can buy and sell currencies of other countries. In bullion markets, gold is bought and sold. Commodities market deals with any type of commodities including bullion, silver, etc. In a nutshell, Share Market, Commodities Market, Bullion Market, Call Money Market, Treasury Bill Market, etc., are the various financial markets.

1.4. Financial Instruments

As is the case with financial markets, financial instruments are dime a dozen. Some of the most well-known ones are: Shares, Debentures, Bonds, Government Securities, Treasury Bills and Commercial Papers. In fact Fixed Deposit Receipts and bonds are also nothing but financial instruments. Incidentally, a check/ cheque or a demand draft drawn in one's favour is also a financial instrument.

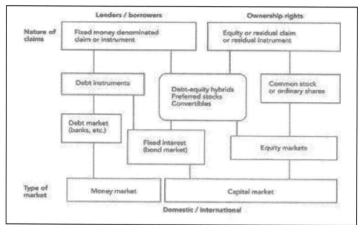

Figure 3 – Financial Markets

1.5. Financial Services

These are services rendered by heterogeneous agencies in the financial system. While these agencies themselves do not accept deposits or lend money, their services are related to financial activity. Such services are essential for the smooth functioning of the very financial system. For example, credit rating. It is a sophisticated and an essential service that is integral to any developed financial system. Similarly, broking and other similar services come under the banner 'financial services'. Some of the banking services out-sourced to other agencies. They can also be classified under financial services.

1.6. Banks and their Uniqueness

Even as one talks about the various components of the financial system, the focus here is on financial intermediaries and, in particular, **banks**. Among all financial institutions in the system, banks stand out, since, they discharge two unique and critical functions, which no other type of financial institution can ever think of. In addition to accepting deposits, the major functions of a bank are - Credit Creators, Money Creators and acting as Payment Conduits. Out of these the last two are unique to banks and no other financial institution can do these roles. That is how a Bank is defined under Banking Regulation Acts of every country. Hence the major functions of a bank can be summarised as:

- An institution that deals in money & its substitutes
- Provides a variety of financial services.
- Accepts deposits from general public
- Issues checking/ savings accounts/ Term deposit accounts
- Extends credit to individuals and businesses
- Facilitates money transactions such as wire transfers, cashier's checks, etc.
- Issues credit cards, ATM, and debit cards
- Provides ancillary services like Safe deposit lockers for storing valuables, financial consulting, etc.
- Derives a profit from the difference in the interest rates paid and charged, respectively

1.6.1.   Banks as Payment Conduits

In the entire financial system, it is only banks that can move money from place to place and from person to person. In other words, they are the backbone of the very Payment System. To put it simply, it would be impossible to move money from one place to another without involving one or more banks in the act. In other words, one just cannot move money by ignoring banks altogether. Of course, apparently, one can think that he/ she has moved money without involving one or more banks. But, in nitty-gritty terms, let us make it clear: "No bank, No movement of money". (The only exception can be, of course, moving physical cash). This unique ability to move money makes banks possibly the most vital part of the financial system.

1.6.2.   Banks as Credit-Creators/ Money-Creators

Besides moving money, banks also enjoy uniqueness. Not only can they extend credit, they can also influence the money supply. This is a function which no other financial institution or intermediary can replicate. This unique capacity of banks to create credit/ deposit itself is an outcome of the fact that they offer negotiable instruments like cheques, demand drafts, etc.

By their ability to create demand deposits and credit, banks are in a position to directly influence the quantum of money that is available in the economy. This means, if one is seriously interested in influencing the money supply in the economy, one need to regulate and control banks. The degree to which, banks can add 'money' is inversely proportional to the cash reserve and other reserves maintained by them. The more the banks maintain as reserve, either voluntarily or because of statutory stipulation, the less is their ability to create deposit money/ credit and vice versa.

1.7. Central Banking - Functions

In almost all the countries, central bank is the pivot of the financial system. The central bank of the country is responsible for maintaining the stability of the financial system. While some of the functions of central banks vary from country to country, the following could be listed as the generic ones:

- Currency Issue
- Bankers' Bank
- Banker to Government
- Supervision of Banks
- Regulation of Credit
- Regulation of Foreign Exchange
- Lender of Last Resort

In most countries, it is the central bank that has monopoly over issue of currencies and coins. In India, Reserve Bank of India is the sole currency issuing authority. Only it can put into circulation currency notes of all denominations. Of course, in the case of one rupee notes and coins, the issuing authority is the Ministry of Finance, but again they are also put into circulation only through the RBI. By the way, there are also countries where central banks have nothing to do with currency issue.

Currency Issue in Hong Kong – While currency issue comes the under the purview of the Central Bank in most countries, this is not to be taken as a universal dictum. There are countries, where central bank does not have any actual issue of currencies. The classic example, in this regard, is Hong Kong. Here, day-to-day currency issue does not come within the purview, of Monetary Authority, the country's central bank. Instead, it is handled by two large commercial banks, viz., Standard Chartered and HSBC. There is no absolute limit set, on the quantum, of Hong Kong Dollar (HKD) that can be issued by these two banks. But the cap comes in the form of a mandatory requirement as per which before putting into circulation each HKD, these two banks need to have in their kitty a particular amount of USD in a prescribed ratio. In technical terms, such a system is known as Currency Board mechanism. Hong Kong is one of the very few countries in the world to follow such a mechanism. Some other countries are: Latvia, Lithuania.

Besides being responsible for currency issue, Central Banks in most of the countries also act as bankers to commercial banks. This means, banks are entitled to maintain their accounts with the Central Bank. In fact, in India and in most other countries, it is mandatory that banks, which participate in the clearing system, should maintain their accounts with the central bank or one of its agent institutions.

In addition to acting as banker to banks, Central Banks also function as banker to the Government. Thus, in India, RBI is the banker to both the Central Government and all the State Governments. In most countries, Central Banks are responsible for the regulation and supervision of Commercial Banks. Similarly, most central banks also regulate extension of credit by banks. Such a regulation could relate to direction of credit, its quantum and/ or its price. In fact, even some of the developed countries have a subdued form of credit regulation by central banks. Incidentally, in the Indian context, banks are mandated by the RBI to ensure that 40 per cent of their credit goes to those borrowers who are classified as priority sector.

Similarly, in those countries where there is restrictions vis-à-vis the use, of foreign exchange, it is more often the Central Bank that regulates such use.

In almost all the countries, Central Bank is responsible for framing monetary policy as well as its implementation. It is through such a periodic policy pronouncements and the related action that Central Banks try to influence the general interest rates and the level of activity in the economy. The Central Banks come out with such a monetary policy twice a year — say April and October – start of summer and monsoon.

Yet another role most Central Banks perform is to act as the lender of last resort to banks during times of crisis (which is the case since 2007 in most of US and Europe regions). There are very few Central Banks that explicitly rule out playing such a role. Thus, when a particular bank or a large number of banks are in a crisis, they can approach the central bank for liquidity support.

1.8. Banking System in Major Countries

Overall banking system across the globe is the same. However, there are some minor differences in the operation of the system between country to country depending on the environment.

1.8.1. Banking System - India

Indian Banking System is fairly complex because of the presence of a variety of banks and a phenomenal number of branches. (Possibly; in terms of sheer branch network, Indian banking system could be reckoned as the largest in the world. Incidentally, State Bank of India (SBI) is the largest bank in terms of number of branches/ personnel. As for the structure, the Ministry of Finance is the super-regulator in as much as RBI itself comes under it. And RBI is the regulator of the banking system in India. It is responsible for bank licensing, as well as branch licensing, issuing directives and supervising the functioning of banks. It is empowered with punitive powers that can be exercised against errant banks. Besides the RBI, there are agencies such as the Deposit Insurance Corporation & Guarantee Corporation of India (DICGC) and the Banking Ombudsman that have jurisdiction over banks in select matters.

1.8.1.1. Categories of banks in India:

Because of the size of the country and to cater different levels of population, different types of banks do co-exist in India. The major categories are:

- Public Sector Banks
- Old Private Sector Banks
- New Private Sector Banks – the new private sector banks started in early 90s are more tech savvy and hence they are classified separately
- Foreign Banks
- Co-operative Banks
- Local Area Banks
- Regional Rural Banks.

Public sector banks themselves could be bifurcated into two categories: SBI & its associates and nationalised banks (such as Canara Bank, UCO Bank, Syndicate Bank, etc.). Old private sector banks are those that are in the private sector, but which came into being before 1992 (Karur Vysya Bank, Federal Bank, Catholic Syrian Bank, etc.). Inversely, those private sectors that got incorporated after 1992 are branded as "New Private Sector Banks". Some of the new private sector banks are: HDFC Bank, ICICI Bank and Indusind Bank. Foreign banks are those that are incorporated outside India but carry on their operations in India under license from the RBI (Citibank, Standard Chartered, HSBC Bank, etc.)

While the above categories of banks are treated as 'commercial banks', there are also other banks in India such as Cooperative Banks, Local Area Banks and Regional Rural Banks. The regulatory framework could vary in detail from one category of banks to another.

1.8.2. Banking System – UK

In the UK, banks that deal with the public are called 'high Street banks'. They take care of the transactional requirements of the general public. Besides, there is a unique institution by name 'Discount House' operating in the UK. A 'discount house' does not deal with the general public at all.

Instead, it is primarily focused on dealing with banks and other financial institutions. On the regulatory front, while till a decade back, it was the Bank of England that was the regulator of the banking system, now that role is being performed by the Financial Supervision Authority (FSA).

1.8.3. Banking System – US

The US banking system is possibly the most fractured/ fragmented system one can find anywhere in the world. In the first place, there are a number of types of banks in the US: International banks, National banks, State banks and Unit banks. Besides, the number of banking entities is phenomenally large in the US (around 12,000). On the regulatory front, these banks/ banking entities are governed by a battalion of regulators. What is more, within the US itself, banking regulations differ from state to State. While till a few years back, the US banking laws were totally anti-competitive, some of the new regulations put in place during and after 1999 may trigger consolidation of banks in the country.

1.9. Credit Unions

A **Credit Union** is a cooperative financial institution that is owned and controlled by its members. Credit unions differ from other financial institutions (banks, savings and loan, etc.) in that the members who have accounts in the Credit Union are the owners of the Credit Union.

Policies of the Credit union governing interest rates and other matters are set by a voluntary Board of Directors elected by and from the membership itself. Only a member of a Credit Union may deposit money or borrow money from it. As such, Credit Unions have historically marketed themselves as providing superior member service and being committed to helping members improve their financial health.

Credit unions typically pay higher dividend (interest) rates on shares (deposits) and charge lower interest on loans than banks. Credit union revenues (from loans and investments) do, however, need to exceed operating expenses and dividends (interest paid on deposits) in order to maintain capital and solvency.

Due to their status as not-for-profit financial institutions, Credit Unions in the United States are exempt from Federal and State income taxes. Credit unions exist in a wide range of sizes, ranging from volunteer operations with a handful of members, to institutions with several billion dollars in assets and hundreds of thousands of members.

1.10.　Non-Banking Financial Corporations (NBFCs)

Non-Bank Financial Companies (NBFCs) also known as **Non-Banks** are financial institutions that provide banking services without meeting the legal definition of a Bank, i.e. one that does not hold a banking license. Regardless of this, its operations are still exercised under the Banking regulation. However this depends on the jurisdiction, as in some jurisdictions, such as New Zealand, any company can do the business of banking, and there are no banking licenses issued.

Non-Bank institutions frequently acts as suppliers of loans and credit facilities, supporting investments in property, providing services such as funding private education, wealth management and retirement planning. However they are typically not allowed to take deposits from the general public and have to find other means of funding their operations such as issuing debt instruments like bonds, loans, commercial papers, etc.

1.11.　Chapter - SUMMARY

- Financial system is an aggregation of institutions, instruments, markets and services that enables smooth movement of money from the savers to the users so that it can be used in an economically advantageous way.
- Financial institutions can broadly be classified as intermediaries, non-intermediaries and regulatory agencies. While an intermediary accepts deposits from savers and lends the same to the users of money, a non-intermediary funds projects, but without taking deposits from savers. Regulatory agencies are responsible for regulating the players in the system.

- Of all the financial institutions, Banks are unique for two reasons. One they can act as payment conduits and two they are also capable of creating credit and thus influencing the overall money supply in the economy.
- In most countries, Central Bank is the pivot of the Financial system. It is responsible for currency issue, besides acting as banker to banks and Governments. It may also supervise banks and may also on the role of lender of last resort in case of need.
- In India, there are different types of banks in the system: Public sector banks, old private sector banks, new private sector banks, foreign banks, cooperative banks, regional rural banks and local area banks. While RBI is the nodal regulator, the regulatory framework it uses could vary according to bank type.
- A Bank is a financial institution that accepts deposits and channels the money into lending activities. The essential function of a bank is to provide services related to the storing of deposits and extending of credit.
- Banking activities can be characterised as Retail banking and Investment banking. Most banks are profit-making, private enterprises. However, some are owned by government, or are non-profit organisations. In some jurisdictions retail and investment activities have been, separated by law.
- Banks in operation today can be broadly classified as Retail Banks or Commercial Banks, Community development Banks, Private Banks, Postal Savings Banks, Regular Savings Banks, Investment Banks, & Merchant Banks.
- Commercial banks also known as Retail Banks provide Products and activities dealing directly with individuals, small businesses and Corporate. Investment Banks are those that provide investment related services and Merchant Banks are traditionally banks engaged in trade financing providing capital to firms in the form of shares rather than loans.
- Universal Banks are large financial services conglomerates that combine commercial banking and investment banking, and sometimes insurance. In recent years, the lines between the two types of structures namely Commercial Banks & Investment

Banks have blurred and almost all large financial institutions have diversified and engage in multiple activities.

- Islamic banks adhere to the concepts of Islamic law. Islamic banking revolves around well-established concepts which are based on Islamic canons.

*****

Chapter 2.   Retail Banking Products and Customers

The term retail is commonplace. Thankfully this obviates the need for defining it. And banking – anyway known by all. In this context let us take the simple definition as accepting deposits for the purpose of lending/ investments. Combining the two, one can say, retail banking should encompass all possible varieties of transactions banks have with their individual customers, catering to the latter's various banking needs. Transactions under retail banking would include acceptance of deposits from individuals, maintaining their accounts and extending loans and advances to them under different schemes. On the services front, issuance of demand drafts, execution of money transfer requests from individual customers and carrying out their standing orders come within the domain of retail banking.

2.1. Dimensions of Retail Banking

Retail Banking can be decomposed into three major compartments, viz.

- ➢ Deposits
- ➢ Credit
- ➢ Services

While this chapter deals with Deposits, the following chapters will deal with Retail Lending (Credit) and other services. Besides, given the fact that Cards and Automated Teller Machines (ATMs) are primarily used by retail customers, the associated operations are also dealt with in the following chapters. At the end of it, a snapshot of the very features of retail banking has to be taken. Besides, a glimpse of private banking to understand its unique features can be had. Also a limited focus on the school of Islamic Banking, an upcoming banking practice in certain countries is seen. Incidentally, some of the topics that get covered are not exactly exclusive to retail banking; instead, they have relevance to across all segments of banking.

2.1.1   Types of Deposits

Deposits can broadly be classified into Term/ Time Deposits and Demand Deposits.

The major products under each head are:

- Demand Deposits
    - o   Statement Savings
    - o   Passbook Savings
    - o   Checking account
    - o   Club Account
    - o   Association accounts
    - o   Money Market Accounts
    - o   Non-resident Accounts
    - o   Current Account (mostly relating to businesses)
    - o   Matured term deposits
- Term Deposits
    - o   Fixed Deposits with interest payable monthly, quarterly, half-yearly or yearly
    - o   Cumulative/ Re-investment Deposits
    - o   Recurring Deposits
- Sweep accounts – a blend of demand cum Term Deposits

Given the fact that bank customers have diverse requirements, it becomes essential that banks offer different types of deposit accounts. Various features of these diverse deposit accounts are so designed that, in totality, they address the entire need spectrum of the depositor community. From a transactional point of view, one can label the entire gamut of such deposit accounts offered by banks as Savings Accounts, Current Accounts, Recurring Deposit Accounts, Term/ Notice Deposit Accounts, Checking Accounts and Hybrid/ Product Deposit Accounts, etc.

2.1.1.1. Savings Bank Accounts

In some part of the globe these are just called Savings Accounts. These are transaction accounts, in short called SB Accounts, meant mainly for individuals. In fact, in India, as per the extant regulations, business firms cannot have SB accounts in their names at all. Banks used to restrict the number of withdrawals a customer can put through in the SB account. However, stiff competition is ensuring that banks turn a blind eye to this restriction. As far as transactions go, a customer can put through any number of deposit and withdrawal transactions in his/ her account so long as he/ she ensures that there is sufficient balance for taking care of withdrawals. While banks permit customers to draw cheques against the balance available in their SB accounts, in the past, most banks, as a matter of policy, were not entertaining overdrawing in SB accounts. But these are different days! Such SB cheques can be made payable to the account holder himself/ herself or to any other third party. As for interest, the banks are empowered to decide the rate of interest. As of now, they cannot discriminate between customers when it comes to quoting SB interest rates. The only exception is, banks can pay a higher interest rate for SB accounts maintained by their staff members.

Earlier, in India, the interest on Savings accounts was being calculated on monthly products by taking consideration the minimum balance between 10th and month-end. But, recently this has been modified to calculate the interest on day's product. Also the interest is compounded on half yearly basis. One serious restriction associated with SB accounts is the fact that in such accounts a customer cannot deposit cheques originally drawn in favour of a third party but subsequently endorsed to him/ her. From the account maintaining bank's point of view, next to Current Accounts, SB accounts are highly transaction-intensive. Banks do levy some charges if stipulated minimum balance is not maintained in the account. In general the method of interest calculation and charges for minimum balance, etc., is the same across the globe may be with subtle differences.

2.1.1.2. Current Accounts

These are also transaction and convenience accounts, primarily meant for the business segment. However, a good number of individuals also maintain current accounts with banks. Banks permit any number/ amount of deposits and withdrawals in current accounts. The only condition is, at any point, for every cheque issued, there should be adequate funds available in the account. Such funds can be that of the depositor or derived from a credit facility/ limit extended by the bank. Unlike in the case of Savings accounts, in current accounts customers can deposit third party cheques endorsed to them. In fact, this is the most significant distinguishing feature between current accounts and Savings accounts. As current accounts are meant for businesses mostly, such a feature needs to be there. Regarding interest payment on current account, the stipulations vary from country to country. In general no interest is payable for current accounts. On the contrary some service charges are levied depending on the number of transactions and minimum balance maintained in the account. However, one understands, payment of interest in respect of current accounts is permissible in Japan. Similar is the case with current accounts maintained with building societies — like Housing Finance Companies — in the UK. From the account-maintaining bank's point of view, current accounts are the most transaction-intensive ones and the average value of such individual current account transactions is generally more than those that go through Savings Accounts. In the Indian context, balances in current accounts are interest-free source of funds for the banks. Thus, for the account maintaining bank, the more is the share of current account deposits, the less is its cost of funds.

2.1.1.3. Term/ Notice Deposits

Under Term Deposit (otherwise also called Fixed deposit), a customer can park his/ her funds with the bank for a fixed period. At the time of depositing itself, both the customer and the bank agree on the tenure of the deposit as well as the rate of interest payable on it. In India, as of now, the minimum period for term deposit is 7 days. In other words, banks cannot accept term deposits for a period less than this timeframe. (But it does not mean a bank has to necessarily accept 7 day deposits)! Going by the available information, one can say there is no restriction whatsoever on the maximum tenure of term deposits. However, for certain business reasons, most banks do not take deposits for any period horizon exceeding 3 years excepting deposits in the name of minors.

As for the interest rate payable on term deposits, in the Indian context, it is now entirely upto individual banks to decide. This means, different banks can quote different rates for term deposits. Also the rate can vary from term to term. It can be either fixed or floating. Nonetheless, for a given term, a bank is prohibited from quoting varying interest rates to different customers. There are some exceptions to this "Interest Parity" principle. Banks are at liberty to quote different rates when a single term deposit amount exceeds a threshold limit say, ₹15 lacs. Besides, banks can quote different rates to different customers when they are taking deposits of tenure between 7 and 15 days. Also banks in India are allowed to pay additional interest rate for those customers who are senior citizens (say above 60 years). Similarly, banks can pay a higher rate on deposits placed by their own staff members. Such minor deviations or exceptions are in vogue in different countries.

As for periodicity of interest payment, it is upto the customer to decide. He/ She may choose to receive interest periodically or would like the same to be accumulated and paid along with the principal amount on the maturity date. Depending upon the choice exercised, the deposit would be christened either non-cumulative or cumulative.

Notice Deposits are somewhat different in their operational details. Here, a customer deposits money with his/ her bank without specifying any fixed period and agrees to serve a notice of a fixed number of days (say, 15 days) before withdrawing his/ her money. Hence, in essence, what is agreed upon in the beginning is not the total period for which the deposit would run, but the notice period for withdrawing money. Notice deposits too carry interest for the actual period for which they have run. While the banks are not legally liable to pre-maturely close the term deposits, banks do help the customers, who are in urgent need of money by paying it before the maturity date. Also banks do lend money against the Fixed Deposit receipts with a slightly higher rate of interest.

2.1.1.4. Recurring Deposits

These accounts are tailor-made for periodic savings by, mostly, individual customers. In these accounts, customers are expected to deposit a fixed sum every week/ month/ quarter. On the contracted maturity date, bank returns the accumulated principal along with interest. As would be obvious from the above, Recurring Deposit accounts are not designed for transaction purposes; instead, they are principally meant for periodic savings.

2.1.1.5. Checking Deposits/ Accounts

These are the most common form of deposit accounts abroad. In the US and Japan, for instance, the term "checking account" refers to any account that can be operated using cheques (or checks?). Given their features, checking accounts are meant for transaction purposes. Customers can put through any number of deposits and withdrawals in such accounts. Depending upon the terms of the contract, banks may or may not pay interest on the balances maintained in checking accounts. Sometimes, banks charge a fee for certain kinds of transactions put through by customers in their checking accounts.

If one were to relate checking accounts to the Indian context, one can say that Savings accounts are equivalent *avatars* of interest bearing checking accounts, while non-interest bearing checking accounts and current accounts seem like, more or less, identical twins. There could be a lot of variants within the very checking account species. Thus, one may come across vanilla checking accounts or basic checking accounts with very few frills, likewise, there are checking accounts targeted primarily at the senior citizens and others at the student community.

2.1.1.6. Resident Foreign Currency Deposits (RFCD)

Introduced in early 00s, in India, these are current accounts that can be maintained by residents in designated foreign currencies, viz., USD,

Japanese Yen, Euro or Pound Sterling. Any legitimate foreign exchange receipt (income or gift) or savings can be credited into the RFCD accounts. Of course, since these are maintained as current accounts, there would be no interest payment whatsoever. These accounts are primarily meant for those residents who have foreign currency income. Such accounts can prove advantageous for the holders when the related foreign currency appreciates in value against Indian Rupee.

2.2. Products/ Hybrids

In essence, Products/ Hybrids are not separate deposit accounts. These combine the features of more than one deposit account type discussed above. Similarly, Flexi-Deposits/ Cubic Deposits are clusters of term deposit accounts maintained in the smallest possible denomination. Likewise, Sweep accounts are Savings accounts that have an inbuilt facility to invest the surplus funds in pre-determined investment schemes by sweeping away the excess balances on a day-to-day basis. In case of transactional need, these investments can be liquidated and the money reverse swept into the related Savings Account.

If one were to use a critical bent of mind, he/ she would find that for all their hype and high sounding names, products/ hybrids are just different manifestations of the various core deposit account types. If there is one aspect to note about products/ hybrids, it is a fact that most of these are more or less impossible to offer, in the absence of a very high level of automation/ technological support. In the Indian context, this is the reason why most such product offerings were not in vogue in conventional banking earlier.

2.3. Non-Resident Accounts

In India, Non-resident accounts are opened and maintained by NRIs (NRI has been defined while discussing the type of customers). Majorly three types of non-resident accounts can be operated. These are: Non-Resident Ordinary (NRO) Account, Non-Resident External (NRE) Account and Foreign Currency Non-Resident (FCNR) Account. Incidentally, there is yet another account type that is not exactly a non-resident account but has something to do with the non-resident status of the accountholder, i.e. Resident Foreign Currency (RFC) Account.

2.3.1. Non-Resident External Accounts (NRE)

This is a type of account that can be opened only by NRIs. Credits can be only by way of foreign inward remittances. The only exception is the periodic interest credit by the bank. These accounts can be in the form of Savings/ Current Account/ Term Deposit Account. They are designated and maintained only in Indian Rupees. Account holder is entitled to repatriate the entire balance in the account (including the accumulated interest) in the Forex rate prevailing on the day of repatriation. However, any loss or gain arising out of currency rate fluctuation is borne by the account holder and not by the bank.

2.3.2. Non-Resident Ordinary Accounts (NRO)

Unlike NRE accounts, in the case of NRO accounts, credits can be in the form of foreign inward remittances in any currency as well as domestically generated credits. Periodic rupee interest would be added to arrive at the balance in the accounts. The interest credited is liable for Income Tax (this is applicable even for Savings Accounts). Irrespective of the mode of individual credits, these accounts would be designated and maintained only in Indian Rupees. NRO accounts can be opened in the form of Savings/ Current/ Term Deposits. The balance in such accounts is repatriable outside India with some restrictions.

2.3.3. Foreign Currency Non-Resident External Account (FCNR)

This is a unique type of non-resident account available. Here, the credit ought to be in the form of foreign inward remittance. The only exception is periodic interest credit by the bank, which itself would be in the specified foreign currency. In other words, as far as the customer is concerned, the account is maintained in designated foreign currencies itself. Customers can maintain the account in any one of the four permitted currencies viz., US Dollar, Pound Sterling, Japanese Yen and Euro. By the way, they can remit in one currency and seek the deposit to be maintained in another. In fact, they can remit in a foreign currency that is not one of the permitted currencies and can ask the bank to maintain in one of the four currencies of their choice. Also the country of residence of the customers can be different from their currency choice. Thus, an NRI residing in Tokyo can remit the proceeds in Japanese Yen and ask the bank to open and maintain his/ her FCNR account in Euro.

These accounts can be only in the form of Term Deposits. No Savings or Current Accounts are permissible under the scheme. The entire balance (including the interest credit) in the account is fully repatriable. Any loss or gain arising out of currency rate fluctuation would be borne/ enjoyed by the bank maintaining the account.

2.3.4. Resident Foreign Currency Account (RFC)

In a true sense, this account is not exactly meant for non-residents. This type of deposit account is for those non-residents who have returned to India and have since become residents. They are permitted till a specified time frame to maintain with banks in India, whatever money they have earned abroad. Such accounts can be in the form of Savings, Current or Term Deposits and are designated, as per the choice of the account holder, in any one of the four permitted foreign currencies, namely, US Dollar, Pound Sterling, Japanese Yen and Euro. Balances in RFC accounts are fully repatriable should the account holder decide to migrate abroad again. Any loss or gain arising out of currency rate fluctuation would be borne/ enjoyed by the bank maintaining the account.

2.4. Account Opening and Types of Customers

There are innumerous types of customers and various formalities/ processes for opening of accounts depending on the types of customers.

2.4.1. Account Opening

The first step in the transactional relationship between a bank and customer is the account opening exercise. It is the customer who submits an application for opening an account in his/ her name. In India, as well as in most other countries, banks do not open accounts in the names of strangers. Hence, they insist upon some form of introduction/ identification of the intending account holder by someone who is known to the bank. (The person introducing need not be, though he/ she generally is, the customer of the bank/branch. Nor is he/ she legally liable for any of the actions of the person he/ she is introducing). Again, subject to certain restrictions, such an introduction can also be in the form of passport, driving license, a reputed company's ID card, etc. The reason why banks insist on such introduction/ identification is simple. Else they could become guilty of abetting a crime known as 'Conversion'. By conversion, it is meant that the illegal appropriation by one person of another person's title/ right over an asset. Incidentally, under Anti Money Laundering (AML) regulations, attempts are being made to bring in regulations that would mandate banks to know their customers not just at the time of account opening, but keep knowing them on a daily basis. Christened "Know-Your-Customer (KYC)", it aims to ensure that by constant monitoring banks set themselves in a position to detect **benami**, money laundering and fraudulent transactions in their customers' accounts as and when they happen. Such an exercise, needless to say, has to be totally software/ learning system driven in as much as it would be impossible for bankers to manually keep track of thousands of transactions that are put through in umpteen accounts every day.

2.4.2. Conversion is a Crime

Suppose 'A' finds on the road a cheque for ₹1,00,000/- favouring one 'B'. Driven by greed, 'A' ventures to open an account, impersonating himself as 'B'. The xxx Bank, Chennai branch does not insist on introduction in this case, neither follows the KYC norms and opens the account in the name of 'B'. 'A' now deposits the cheque in the newly opened account. On credit of the proceeds, he withdraws the entire amount of ₹1,00,000/-, all along pretending himself to be 'B' and then vanishes. If and when 'A' gets caught for converting 'B''s title into his own the branch officials of xxx Bank, Chennai Branch too would be implicated for abetting 'conversion' — be abetted, the crime by not verifying whether the person claiming himself to be 'B' was actually 'B'. In other words, he overlooked one critical step in account opening, namely identification/ introduction.

2.5. Joint Accounts

Deposit accounts can be opened in the name of one or more individuals. When a single individual has an account in his/ her name, he/ she can operate the account himself/ herself. However, it is not essential that he/ she alone should operate the account. By executing a power of attorney, he/ she can authorize someone else to operate his/ her account. The possibilities get immense when a deposit account is maintained in the joint names of two or more individuals. Such joint accounts can be operated in different ways:

- Joint Operation
- Either or Survivor
- Former or Survivor
- Latter or Survivor
- Anyone or Survivor(s)

For illustration, let us suppose 'K' and 'A' have a joint account with a bank branch. If the operation style opted by 'K' and 'A' together then the account is "joint operation", both of them have to give all operational instructions together to the bank branch, including issue of cheque. Thus, in this case, every cheque needs to be signed by both 'K' and 'A'. Only then the bank would honour the cheque. On the other hand, if the joint account is maintained in the style "Either or Survivor" **(E-or-S),** then either 'K' or 'A' can give instructions to the bank and the latter would act upon that. Thus, in an **E-or-S** situation, if a cheque is signed by either 'K' or 'A', it would get paid by the bank. Let us further suppose that in the application form for opening the joint account, 'K''s name appears first followed by that of 'A'. In such a situation, 'K' is the 'former' and 'A' is the 'latter'. If the account is styled as "Former or Survivor" **(F-or-S),** the bank would act upon the instruction of 'K' and he alone till he is alive. 'A' can have a say in the operation of the account if and only if 'K' is no more. On the other hand, if the style of operation is "Latter or Survivor" **(L-or-S),** the bank would go by the instruction of 'A' and 'A' alone till he/ she is alive. 'K' can operate the account only on the death of 'A'. In the same fashion, if the account is opened by more than 2 names also called "Anyone or Survivor" **(A-or-S),** instructions are carried out.

Incidentally, it is also possible to have hybrid operating styles in a joint account. Thus, an account can be E-or-S for cheques upto an amount and beyond that the style can be prescribed as 'joint operation'. Regardless of the operating style, for income tax purposes and other legal consequences, in the case of a joint account, going by the extant tax laws, banks in India deem as if the account is in the name of the first named person only.

2.6. Dormancy to be avoided

Banks classify their deposit accounts on the basis of customer triggered activity. This applies to transaction accounts such as Savings and Current Accounts. Most banks designate a Savings or Current Account as dormant in case there is no transaction whatsoever therein for a prescribed period (this period is taken as one year in certain banks). Once an account is designated as dormant, most banks mandate that any fresh transaction affecting that account would have to be approved by a branch senior official after thorough investigation. This is because, a good percentage of frauds that happen in the banking industry predominantly use dormant accounts as their pipeline. As per the extant Indian laws, if an account remains dormant exceeding a certain number of years the balances in the account would have to be transferred to the credit of the Reserve Bank of India. This rule is applicable to matured term deposits also – which are not withdrawn within a time frame from the due date.

2.7. Nomination

Every depositor can designate a nominee who would be eligible to receive the proceeds available in the corresponding account on his/ her demise. Incidentally, as per the statutory provision, in the case of bank deposits, the number of nominees cannot be anything but one. Of course, the same depositor has a right to nominate different nominees for different deposits held by him/ her with the same bank/ branch. On the death of a depositor, the concerned nominee has the right to receive the account proceeds, but no right whatsoever to operate the account concerned.

As soon as a bank pays the deposit proceeds to the nominee concerned, it stands fully discharged and is required to oversee the usage of the proceeds by the nominee even if some conditions have been attached to the usage of such funds by the account holder. Nomination facility eases the otherwise treacherous route legal heirs have to wade through for claiming the deposits of the deceased.

2.8. Different types of Customers

As could imagine, bank customers are heterogeneous. While dealing with certain types of customers, banks have to take additional precautions lest they get into some trouble.

2.8.1. Minors

In the case of minors, banks have to be doubly careful. Of course, there is nothing in the law that prohibits a bank from opening accounts in the name of a minor. In fact, some banks have special deposit schemes targeted at minors. Also banks can allow their minor customers to have chequeable accounts, though the age beyond which a minor customer can issue cheques is generally prescribed to as 10 or 12 years. (Individual banks have discretion to decide this cut-off age). While banks have no hassle in maintaining deposit accounts in the names of minors, at all costs they ensure that they do not permit overdrawing in such accounts even by chance. This is because, as per the English laws, minors can legitimately (and royally!) disown any liability.

Whenever a bank maintains an account in the name of a minor, it needs to diarize the date on which the concerned minor would be attaining majority. The 'majority date' is critical inasmuch as on that date the customer becomes legally qualified to enter into all sorts of contracts. Till such time the account holder is a minor, the account will be operated by the natural/ legal guardian for and on behalf of the minor.

2.8.2. Partnerships

Banks should ensure that the account is operated as per the terms and conditions contained in the Partnership Deed.

2.8.3. Corporates

A corporate has a special entity – not enjoyed by Partnership neither by Sole Proprietorship firms. These are denoted, in different countries as:

- Ltd. (Limited)
- Private [(P), (Pvt)] Ltd. (Private Limited)
- LLC – (Limited Liability Company)
- Inc. – (Incorporated)
- LLP – (Limited Liability Partnership)
- Government Corporations
- Municipalities

The Certificate of Incorporation given by the Registrar of Companies is the birth certificate for the corporate. An account can be opened in the name of a corporate, only if there is a resolution to that effected by the concerned board. Operations in the account should be by those officials authorised in that regard by the board. Besides, any borrowing by a company needs specific approval from the company's board. Similarly, even account closing should be only as per a board resolution.

2.8.4. Non Resident Indians (NRIs)

A non-resident is defined in 2 ways. One by Income Tax (I-T) Rules and other by Foreign Exchange Monitoring Act (FEMA), which is the one binding on banks. However, for academic purpose let us also know what Income Tax Act says – if an assesse stays outside India for more than 180 days in a financial year (assessment year) he is called a **non-resident**.

Under banking rules NRI is – a person, who is out of India for a gainful employment and he/ she should be:

- Of Indian Origin or

- Either of his/ her parents should be of Indian origin or
- Any one of his/ her grandparents should be of Indian origin

2.8.5. Hindu Undivided Families (HUFs)

All transactions should be at the instance of the **Karta** (Karta is the head of the family). Without an express direction from the Karta, no transactions can be put through in the account.

2.8.6. Trusts

It is for the banks to ensure that all transactions in accounts maintained by a trust are in tune with the objectives of the trust and are meant for the advantage of the beneficiary/ beneficiaries named in the trust deed.

2.8.7. Associations

These are non-profit organisations, such as Cosmopolitan Club, Gymkhana Club, etc. Under no circumstance, should a bank extend any credit facility to a club.

2.8.8. Custodian

Custodian is the person who is appointed by court or Government to operate the frozen accounts or ceased accounts. The court order or Government order has to be followed in its entirety.

2.8.9. Illiterates, Purdasin Ladies, Visually Impaired, Lunatics

Normally banks allow the transactions mainly withdrawals based on the customer's signatures on the instruments. The Illiterate or Visually Impaired customers cannot sign the instruments and the banks go by the thumb impressions. In reality the thumb impression is the best and unique identity of a person more than a signature. But it is very difficult to compare 2 thumb impressions through a naked eye. Hence bankers do compare the identity through the photo already provided to them while opening the account. The issue here is that for every transaction the account holder has to visit the branch in person. Especially for the visually impaired customers, banks do take a witness, possibly known to the customer to ensure that the correct amount is disbursed to the concerned customer. In the case of Purdasin Ladies it is all the more difficult to compare with the photo and hence a witness of a person known to the bank is a must. A customer, if he is Lunatic, the account opening and all the transactions can happen only when he is in a sensible state of mind and with a strong witness. The specialty of these types of customers is that the transaction can happen only in person in front of a bank official and not through a third person or through a cheque.

2.8.10. Banks

Every bank do maintain account with one or other banks for their own transactions. Hence Bank is a special type of customer for another bank. The bank issues power of attorney to its officials to operate such accounts with other banks. The bank maintaining the account of another bank should go by the power of attorney issued by the employer. It clearly mentions the delegated power and the amount of and nature of transaction the official can put through.

2.9. Chapter - SUMMARY

- Retail banking deal with individual customers be it deposits or lending.
- Retail banking encompasses all possible varieties of transactions banks have with their individual customers, catering to the latter's various banking needs. In a broad sense, there are three dimensions to retail banking: Deposits, Retail Credit and Services.
- Banks offer Savings, Current, Term Deposit and Recurring Deposit Accounts to their retail customers. Banks also tailor deposit products combining the features of more than one deposit account type for offer to their customers.
- Banking customers are of many a type – Minors, Sole Proprietorship Firms, Partnership firms, Corporates – Ltd., (P) Ltd, LLP, etc., NRIs, HUFs, Trusts, Associations, Custodians, Illiterates, Purdasin Ladies, Visually Impaired, Lunatics, Banks, etc.

*****

Chapter 3.   Negotiable Instruments

A **negotiable instrument** is a document guaranteeing the payment of a specific amount of money, either on demand, or at a set time. According to the Section 13 of the Negotiable Instruments Act, 1881 in India, a negotiable instrument means a promissory note, bill of exchange or cheque payable either to order or to bearer. Hence, there are just three types of negotiable instruments such as promissory note, bill of exchange and cheque. Cheque also includes Demand Draft.

More specifically, it is a document contemplated by a contract, which:

- Warrants the payment of money, the promise of or order for conveyance of which is unconditional
- Specifies or describes the payee, who is designated on and memorialised by the instrument and
- Is capable of change through transfer by valid negotiation of the instrument.

As payment of money is promised subsequently, the instrument itself can be used by the holder in due course as a store of value; although, instruments can be transferred for amounts in contractual exchange that are less than the instrument's face value (known as 'discounting'). Under United States law, Article 3 of the Uniform Commercial Code as enacted in the applicable State law governs the use of negotiable instruments, except banknotes ("Federal Reserve Notes", aka "paper dollars").

3.1. Financial Instruments

Bankers deal with a deluge of instruments. Of these the most important ones are:
- Cheques
- Demand Drafts
- Pay Orders/ Banker's Cheque/ Cashier's Cheque
- Bills of Exchange
- Promissory Notes

In the case of all these Instruments there are different players like:

- Drawer – The person who writes the instrument
- Drawee – The person in whose favour the payment instruction is conveyed
- Payee or Beneficiary – The person who stands to gain from the instrument.
- Endorser – one who signs and delivers the instrument
- Endorsee – one who gets the endorsed instrument

3.1.1.   Cheque

This is also called as check in US and in some countries. When a cheque is drawn, it is an instruction to the bank/ branch by the drawer to pay a certain sum of money to a specified person viz. drawee. Deriving from the above, it can be said that a cheque is nothing but a Bill of Exchange[1] drawn on a bank by one of its depositors. Here the drawer, in other words the writer of the cheque, is the account holder. The bank branch is the drawee, as it has to observe the instruction given through the cheque. And the payee is the person to whom the cheque is made payable.

3.1.2.   Demand Draft

In simple terms, a demand draft is nothing but a Bill of Exchange drawn by one of the branches of a bank on another branch of its own[2]. It is an order issued by one branch of a bank on another branch. Suppose a student, 'S', go to the Chennai branch of XYZ Bank, pay money and obtain a demand draft for ₹10,000/- in favour of University of Delhi payable at its New Delhi branch. Here the Chennai branch is giving instruction to the New Delhi branch to pay University of Delhi ₹10,000/-. Hence, the former branch is the drawer; the latter branch is the drawee and University of Delhi is the payee. What about 'S' - he happened to be the purchaser of the demand draft. Her name may not even figure in the instrument.

---

[1] Discussed below in this chapter
[2] Sometimes it is another bank with which the drawer bank has relationship

3.1.3.   Pay Order/ Banker's Cheque/ Cashier's Cheque

A commonplace instrument, Pay Order is also known by different names viz., Banker's Cheque, Manager's Cheque, Cashier's Cheque, etc. A pay order can be treated as a Promissory Note[3] issued by a bank branch undertaking/ agreeing to pay a certain sum of money to the payee. In the more realistic sense it is a demand draft – an order issued by a bank branch on itself. Suppose another student 'B' walks in the Chennai branch of ABC Bank, pay money and purchases a pay order for ₹10,000/- in favour of University of Madras. Here ABC Bank, Chennai is the drawer as well as the drawee. University of Madras is the payee and 'B' is the purchaser.

3.1.4.   Bills of Exchange

A bill of exchange is an instrument that contains an order given by the creditor to the debtor asking the latter to pay a certain sum of money either on demand or on a specified future date. Here the creditor writes the instrument and hence he/ she is the drawer. And the instrument is drawn on the debtor who needs to comply with its instruction. Hence, he/ she becomes the drawee. The payee is the creditor who is supposed to get the proceeds of the bill. Bills of exchange form the backbone of commerce & trade and thus, are also the main diet of corporate banking/ trade financing.

3.1.5.   Promissory Note

Commonly called Pro-Note, this contains a promise by the debtor to pay on demand or on a specified date a certain sum of money to the creditor whose name is indicated in the instrument. The debtor also undertakes to pay interest at a prescribed percentage. In the case of promissory note, the debtor who writes the instrument becomes the drawer. He/ She is also the drawee inasmuch as the instruction in the instrument is to be observed by him and the creditor is the payee. In the case of all their loan transactions, banks get Promissory Notes signed by the respective

---

[3] Discussed below in this chapter

borrowers. The main criterion of the promissory note is that it contains the terms "I promise to pay a sum of .... with interest at the rate of ....".

If the wordings in a currency note is observed keenly – it is also a promise to pay – signed by the Governor of the Central Bank of the country. In that case Is it also a Promissory Note? No – it is **not** – since the currency note is a promise to pay the **bearer** and not to a specific payee. Also it is, by nature, exempted to be a promissory note and hence it is not a negotiable instrument. This will be clearer when the concepts of endorsement and negotiation are understood.

3.2 Endorsement

In banking parlance the above are all negotiable instruments. The meaning of the term negotiation is very simple. A person to whom an instrument is payable can pass on his/ her title to another person just by signing on the reverse and handing over the same. For instance, XYZ issues a cheque for ₹50,000/- favouring ABC. The later may pass on his title over the cheque to PQR just by signing on the reverse of the cheque with or without writing the words "Pay PQR". Endorsement is that simple – what is more, by definition, the process of endorsement conveys a good title to the person getting the instrument technically, 'endorsee') irrespective of the nature of the title of the person endorsing it. Besides, endorsement need not be a one-step affair. In the above case, if desired, PQR can endorse the same cheque to DEF by writing "Pay to DEF" and signing. On his part, DEF may further endorse the cheque further to GHI and so on. And this process can go on indefinitely. In other words, there is no limit to the number of times an instrument cheque can be endorsed. The only practical limit is the availability of space on the reverse side of the cheque. But the law gives a workaround to overcome this limitation by attaching a white sheet as an annexure to the instrument in question, which is called "Alonge" and carry out his/ her endorsement there.

3.3 Crossing — Styles & Significance

An instrument that carries no crossing across its face is an "open instrument". In such a case, the payee can make the payment in cash across the counter. However, the moment an instrument is crossed in one way or the other, a negative condition gets added, prohibiting such across-the-counter cash payment. Besides, such a crossing itself can be in different styles and each has a particular significance.

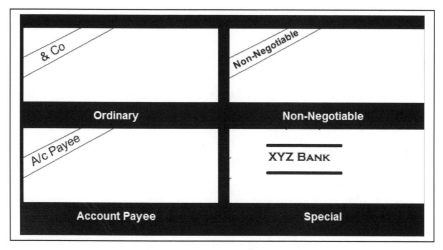

Figure 4 – Types of crossing

3.3.1   Ordinary Crossing

When two parallel lines are drawn across the face of the cheque (with or without the phrase "& Co"), the instrument is said to be ordinarily crossed. The only restriction of such a crossing is that the proceeds of the instrument cannot be paid in cash.

3.3.2   Account Payee Crossing

When an instrument carries across its face two parallel lines with the phrase "account payee" or "account payee only" inscribed on it, the instrument gets **Account Payee** crossing very restrictive in its nature. In such a case, the proceeds cannot be paid in cash. Besides, such an instrument cannot be endorsed at all to anybody. All these mean, the proceeds of the instrument can be credited only to the account of the person whose name is indicated as the drawee. In fact, such a style of crossing is possibly a safe way of paying through cheque. Incidentally this crossing is not dealt with by Negotiable Instruments Act 1881. However, this has been in vogue and hence has become acceptable practice by banks.

3.3.3 Special Crossing

When a cheque carries across its face two parallel lines with the name of a bank inscribed in between, then it is supposed to be "specially crossed". In such an instance, the condition is that the cheque has to be paid through that specified bank only.

3.3.4 Non-Negotiable Crossing

When a cheque is crossed and carries between the two lines the term "Non-Negotiable", it is a cautionary crossing. While such a crossing does not restrict endorsement/ negotiation of the cheque by one party to another, the ultimate beneficiary of the instrument cannot get a title that is in any way better than that of any of the other endorsees. If, for instance, one of the endorsees in the chain had stolen the cheque, then the ultimate beneficiary's title would equally be defective. In fact, it is advisable not to accept a non-negotiable cheque endorsed.

As could be seen from the above, one advantage which crossing entails is that it negates across the counter cash payment of the proceeds of the cheque. This means, there is a definite payment trail once a cheque is crossed. Thus, in case of any fraudulent encashment, it would be possible to identify the account/ person responsible for it. Incidentally, in the Indian context, as per the Income Tax laws, it is mandatory that any payment to a third party beyond a cut -off amount needs to be effected only by way of a crossed instrument. By the way it is not essential that a cheque is to be crossed only by the issuer/ drawer of the cheque. Anyone can at any time-cross a cheque.

3.4 Chapter Summary

Negotiable instruments are the back-bone of the entire financial system, more so for the banking system. There are different types of negotiable instruments used across.

- Cheques
- Demand Drafts
- Pay Orders/ Banker's Cheque/ Cashier's Cheque
- Bills of Exchange
- Promissory Notes

The different stakeholders of negotiable instruments are:

- Drawer – The person who writes the instrument
- Drawee – The person in whose favour the payment instruction is conveyed
- Payee or Beneficiary – The person who stands to gain from the instrument.
- Endorser – one who signs and delivers the instrument
- Endorsee – one who gets the endorsed instrument

The instruments can be crossed to restrict its playability. Various types of crossing are:

- Ordinary/ Special Crossing
- Account payee crossing/ Not Negotiable Crossing

*****

Chapter 4.   Retail Lending

Lending in banking parlance is also called as Credit (this should not be confused with Debit/ Credit in accounting). Also the loans forms part of assets side of the balance sheet[4] and hence sometimes referred as assets.

Retail credit refers to the portfolio of small value, but large volume loans extended by banks to individuals and in some cases to small businesses also. Such loans are not homogeneous in their nature. In fact, there are quite many variants among them, each meeting different kinds of financial requirements of individual customers.

4.1   Features of Retail Credit

There are certain unique features associated with retail credit. In the first place, loans under the retail umbrella are small in value, but are large in number. The latter fact makes the portfolio as a whole transaction-intensive. Besides retail loans need to be of different varieties in order to meet the entire spectrum of the financial needs of individuals. This calls for the introduction of a large number of loan products on the retail front. From a business point of view as a portfolio, retail loans are far more stable, adding solidity to a bank's business. On the 'returns' front, retail loans are extremely attractive. Besides, retail loans function as good portfolio balancers, especially when a bank is already having a large exposure to corporates. As for recovery efforts, the retail loans may call for extensive follow up and recovery. One favourable point about retail credit is that it has the potential to make the bank develop lifetime business relationship with individuals by its ability to meet the needs of individuals at various points in their lifetime.

---

[4] Discussed in detail in balance sheet chapter

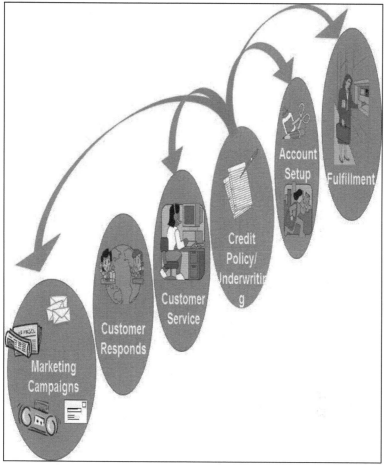

Figure 5 – Retail Credit Process

The above diagram explains the different stages of retail credit process. Let us understand more in this regard.

4.2   Some Credit Concepts

Some of the credit concepts are explained below. This will enable clear understanding of the types of credit, appraisal process, etc.

4.2.1. Credit Scoring

Regardless of whether the appraisal process is manual or automated, in the retail front, most banks use a framework by name "Credit Scoring" to evaluate individual proposals. Under this, marks are assigned to various parameters/ attributes that find a place in the proposal. And using varying weights for different parameters, an aggregate score, otherwise called "Credit Score" is arrived at for individual borrowers. If the Credit Score is more than the minimum threshold acceptable, the proposal is sanctioned. Conversely, if the Credit Score for a particular borrower is less than the minimum threshold, then the proposal stands rejected.

4.2.1.1. DMS vs. DSS

Having a credit scoring model in place makes retail credit decision that much easier. Nonetheless, when banks use automated credit scoring, they may end up in the horns of a dilemma whether to use the same as a Decision Making System (DMS) or Decision Support System (DSS). If it were to be a DMS, effectively there would be no decision making role at all for the retail credit manager. He/ she becomes a mere spectator to the entire process of credit sanction. On the other hand, if the automated appraisal system were to be just a DSS, then all credit decisions have to be finally taken by the credit manager, which may negate the very purpose of automation. One way to resolve this DMS-DSS dilemma could be to keep the system DMS *vis-à-vis* those proposals that have very high or very low credit scores and let the system refer other proposals to the credit manager where the credit scores come in the grey area. In such limited and borderline cases, the individual retail credit manager may apply his/ her mind, exercise his/ her discretion and arrive at a final decision.

4.2.1.2. Credit Scoring — Static and Dynamic Models

Credit scoring models can be designed to be static or dynamic. In the case of a static model, the various parameters for which scores are to be assigned as well as the weights to be reckoned for each such parameter are pre-defined/ hard-coded. Hence, such a model cannot, on its own, modify the parameters or the weights. In other words, such a model would be too rigid to be of real use. On the contrary, dynamic credit scoring models need to be learning systems driven. Such a credit scoring model keeps assessing on an on-going basis the transactional behavior of various individual borrower accounts already sanctioned/ disbursed. On the basis of its observations, it checks whether the parameters currently being used are relevant and whether any new ones need to be used. Also the current weights are reviewed and modified when and where necessary. Such an automatic review and updation of the model can be designed to be carried out either periodically or on a real time basis. Given the system load, a periodic updation looks desirable. Nonetheless, individual banks may have different preferences in this regard.

4.2.2. Interest Rate

In respect of loans, there are many ways of charging interest. Some of methods highly in vogue globally are:

- Fixed
- Floating
- Cap
- Floor
- Collar

Fixed Rate of Interest – In the case of fixed rate contract, the rate of interest payable by the borrower would remain the same throughout the tenure of the loan regardless of what happens to the general market interest rates. By locking to a fixed rate, for sure, the borrower is protecting himself/ herself from the adverse impact of any upward revision in the market rates. But, at the same time, he/ she also forgoes the benefit that could have accrued to him/ her during moments of interest rate fall/ crash.

Floating Rate of Interest – Sometimes, the bank and/ or the borrower may like to have a floating rate of interest. In such cases, they need to agree on three things. First of all, they should agree on the "benchmark rate"— also called "base rate" or "anchor rate" – with reference to which the interest rate payable by the borrower would float. Such a benchmark rate should be a commonly accepted one. (For instance, it can be LIBOR or SIBOR or MIBOR or PLR of the bank or the Treasury-bill rate. Sometimes, banks may use their own Term Deposit rate as the benchmark rate).

Having fixed the benchmark rate, the bank decides the add-on to the benchmark rate for arriving at the actual rate payable by the borrower. Besides, there is one more thing to be agreed upon. That is the frequency with which the interest rate payable by the borrower would be reset.

Cap – this is a floating rate of interest with a maximum limit fixed, while sanctioning the loan itself, more than which the rate of interest cannot move. This is in a way advantageous to the borrower.

Floor – this is a floating rate of interest with a minimum limit fixed, while sanctioning the loan itself, less than which the rate of interest cannot move. This is in a way advantageous to the bank.

Collar – this is a floating rate of interest with minimum and maximum limits fixed, while sanctioning the loan itself, less or more than which the rate of interest cannot move. This protects the interest of both the bank and the borrower.

4.2.3.   Repayment Methods

As is the case with rate of interest methods, there is many a way, in which the repayment can be structured. Some of them are;

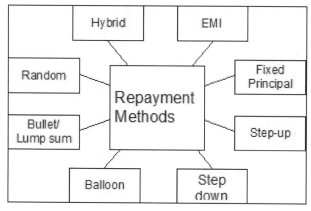

Figure 6 – Repayment Methods

Every method has its pluses and minuses. Whenever the borrower is given the option, he/ she should select the one that suits his/ her present and future cash inflows, other commitments as well as the tax consequences.

Equated Monthly Installment (EMI) – In the case of EMI, for a given principal, RoI and tenor of the loan, the monthly repayment quantum remains constant throughout the period of the loan. With each installment, what changes is the respective proportion of principal and interest. The proportion of interest in the total installment quantum comes down with each installment. Inversely, the proportion of principal component goes up.

Fixed Principal – As the name indicates, what is kept constant in this method is the amount of principal payable during each installment. The interest portion would keep varying. Everything else remaining the same, the absolute quantum of interest component would keep coming down with every installment. Naturally, this implies, the total installment commitment would taper off over time.

Step-up – Under the step-up repayment model, in general the total commitment (interest + principal) gets stepped up in stages. Suppose 'X' is the amount of the first six installments. And from the 7th to 12th installment, the amount is stepped upto '1.2X'. And again from the 13th to

18th installment the commitment gets stepped upto '1.5X' and so on. Step-up model is advantages for those customers who are expecting a steady rise in their disposable income at fixed intervals.

Step-down – This is an exact mirror Image of the step-up method. Here the total commitment is initially set at a higher level. After a certain number of installments, it is brought down by a factor. And again after an equal number of further installments, it is brought down further.

Balloon – This is a very special repayment pattern, not often used in the retail segment. It is more prevalent in corporate banking. Under this, the borrower and the banker agree on the total period within which the loan would be cleared in full. And the borrower keeps paying a notional amount every time till the last installment. The last payment would generally be very huge in comparison to other installments. Balloon type installment scheme is ideal when the borrower is expecting a windfall at the fag end of the repayment period and is not in a position to meet sizeable repayment commitments at present. In some places this method is a blend of step-up and step-down methods. The repayment gradually increases and after some time it decreases.

Bullet/ Lump Sum – Under this method, the borrower gets a certain time for repaying the loan. Till the due date, he/ she keeps paying only the interest portion. And on the final due date, he/she repays the entire principal amount in one shot. Or again the borrower has the right to repay the principal in parts at any point of time during the tenor of the loan. However, he has to repay the interest as and when charged.

Random – As the very name makes it obvious, the repayment pattern is random. Such randomness can relate to two factors: the date/ dates on which various installments would be paid and/or the quantum, of each such installment. Under this method, the borrower repays whatever amount he/ she can and whenever he can. Such a repayment structure is extremely advantageous to the borrower, but can make life tough for the bank.

Hybrid – Occasionally a customer may like to follow a repayment pattern that is a hybrid of any two or more of the methods above. In such situations, banks tailor the repayment schedule to suit his/ her convenience. Such a structure, he/ she may think, may be in tandem with his/ her expected future cash inflows.

It can be noted that at present, all the methods discussed above may not be available in a single country. It is a list of global methods.

4.2.4. Security and Charge Types

While banks may occasionally extend credit sans-security, more often than not they get their lending secured in one way or the other. Such a security can be the very asset being financed by the loan or something else in addition. In the lexicon of some of the banks, when the financed asset itself becomes a security for the loan given, it is called "Primary Security". On the other hand, when an asset that is not financed by the loan becomes an additional security for the loan given, it is christened 'collateral' or "Secondary Security". However, in some of the western banks' context, the term collateral stands for any asset offered as security to the lender.

Charge Type – Security cannot be homogeneous in nature. Depending upon the type of loan being sanctioned, anything from shares to house property to life insurance policy can be offered as security. As the nature of these securities differs, so does the method of establishing the financing banks' rights over them. The following are the generic ways in which banks establish their rights over the securities offered to them.

Pledge – Possibly one of the most common place methods of establishing charge. When an asset is pledged in favour of a bank, the latter would have its physical possession. This automatically rules out the usage of the asset by the borrower during the tenure of the loan. In the retail banking domain, pledge is used in respect of assets such as gold, etc. In case the borrower defaults, under pledge, the bank would have the automatic right to dispose of the asset and use the sale proceeds for wiping off the dues in the borrower's loan account. At the same time, the bank is duty bound to pay to the borrower any sale proceeds received in excess of the loan outstanding. In the case of pledge the possession is with the lender and the ownership lies with the borrower.

Hypothecation – From a legal point of view, hypothecation is as good as pledge. The only difference is in this case the borrower can retain the possession of the asset and use it. In retail banking, vehicles financed stand hypothecated to the bank, not pledged to it. For, if the funded vehicles were to be pledged, borrower cannot use it till he/ she pays the last installment. In the case of hypothecation the possession lies with the borrower and the ownership lies with the lender.

Lien – Banks use lien as a method of establishing their charge in respect of those assets/ valuables that come to their possession in the natural course of their business. This is applicable to the securities like Fixed Deposits of banks or other corporates, shares, etc.

Assignment – Assignment is a process by which the beneficial rights of one person over an asset (claim/ receivable/ contract) get transferred to another. This method of charge is applicable in the case of Life Insurance Policies being offered as security.

Mortgage – Mortgage is always applicable for immovable properties being offered as security. In general, transfer of title/ interest in any immovable property from one person to another is affected by putting through mortgage. Mortgage has a lot of variants within it. In fact, in some of the variants, no actual transfer of title happens at all except in case of need. Of the different variants of mortgages, two are most common:

Registered Mortgage and Mortgage by deposit of title deeds also called as Equitable Mortgage. Under registered mortgage there is an actual transfer of title from one person to another. On the other hand, when an equitable mortgage transaction, is put through, there is no actual transfer at that moment, only an explicit consent by the property owner to handover over the title deed as a security[5].

---

[5] Mortgage as a type of loan discussed later in the same chapter

4.2.5. Technical Terms of Credit

Understand of some technical terms like Limit, Margin, Drawing Power, Liability, Excess Drawing, etc., will make the other discussions more clearer.

Instead of defining the concepts, it is better understood through an example.

A borrower approaches his banker for a car loan – to purchase a car, which costs ₹6,00,000/-.

Even if the borrower is otherwise eligible for a loan of ₹6,00,000/-, the bank may not lend the entire cost of the car. The borrower has to meet some portion of it say 25% viz. ₹1,50,000/-. This amount is called **margin** amount.

The bank sanctions the remaining amount of ₹4,50,000/-. This is the **limit** of the loan beyond which the outstanding cannot go at any point of time. The EMI has been fixed at ₹20,000/- per month.

After two years – the borrower would have paid ₹2,40,000/- and a sum of ₹1,50,000/- has been added as interest. Hence the loan outstanding is:

As on 01st January 2009 – loan sanctioned   ₹4,50,000/- (1)
As on 01st January 2012 – add interest charged so far   ₹1,50,000/- (2)
    Less repayments   ₹2,40,000/- (3)
    Amount **outstanding** (1) + (2) – (3)   ₹3,60,000/-

This amount of ₹3,60,000/- is the **drawing power** or **liability** of the borrower as on 01st January 2012. In this case the liability and the drawing power are equal.

Assuming during these two years, the borrower has repaid only ₹1,40,000/-. The liability would be ₹4,60,000/-. But the drawing power remains the same as ₹3,60,000/-. Hence there is an **excess** or **above the limit** of ₹1,00,000/-. (In practice, if there are dues in repayments, the interest charged would be higher. For simplifying the calculations the interest charged is retained as it is.)

In the first place, a bank fixes the eligible limit for the borrower. This is the maximum permissible outstanding in the account at any point of time. Besides, the bank would also impose a margin requirement (say, 30%) *vis-à-vis* whatever asset that is offered as security for the loan.

In the case of loan accounts, which are meant as running accounts, the maximum permissible outstanding is either the limit or the value of asset/ security minus the margin portion *called drawing power* - whichever is less. Under no circumstances, can the drawing power exceed the limit sanctioned to the borrower. Often, the drawing power keeps varying at very frequent intervals when the borrowing is against certain types of assets like equity shares. On the other hand, the limit remains stable for a fairly long period of time, and only occasionally it is revised either upwards or downwards.

4.3   Retail Credit - Types

Broadly the retail credit portfolio can be divided into **two:**

- Unsecured Loans
- Secured Loans.

4.3.1.   Unsecured Loans

As the very name suggests, these loans are extended by banks to their credit worthy retail customers without any security backing. Examples of Unsecured Loans can be – Personnel Loan, Education Loan, Marriage Loan, etc. More often than not, in such cases, the only comfort available to the bank is the perceived high income/ wealth level of the borrower. Everything else remaining the same, compared to a secured loan, the element of credit risk is more in an unsecured loan. Hence, banks get choosy here. Mostly, professionals with high income levels, employees of reputed corporates, etc., are the preferred targets for these loans.

4.3.2. Secured Loans

Within Secured Loans, there are quite a many variants based on the security against/ purpose for which such loans are extended.

4.3.2.1. Loans against Deposits

Banks also extend loans against their own deposits. This happens when a depositor needs money, but does not want to break or foreclose his deposit account. For the lending bank, for various reasons, lending against its own deposit should be the most comforting thing to happen. In general, in the Indian context, banks charge interest rate which is 2% more than what they pay on the corresponding deposit. Generally, banks do allow a loan amount equivalent to 75% of the deposit amount (inclusive of accrued interest) retaining a margin of 25%.

In the case of loan against deposits, default chances are nil. In fact, these loans can be designed to be self-liquidating in nature. Again, in case of default, the bank can exercise its lien over the deposit and use the proceeds to clear the dues in the loan account. Loans may also be sanctioned by banks against deposits maintained by a customer with other banks. In such cases, however, an extra caution needs to be exercised by the funding bank. That is, to communicate with the bank branch concerned and get its lien registered over the deposit.

4.3.2.2. Loans against Shares

In the retail segment, banks also lend against the security of shares. Such loans, however, come with a list of conditions attached to them. In the first place, banks do not extend this loan facility against any and every company's share traded in the stock markets. Instead each bank has its own list of 'permissible' shares for extension of credit. Only those shares, which enjoy very good liquidity and which are less volatile get a nod for inclusion in the list. Besides, the list is kept dynamic in the sense that banks keep adding and deleting shares from time to time. Moreover, in the case of loans against shares, generally a higher level of margin is prescribed (> 50%) so that the dues to the bank stand fully covered even in the event of a market meltdown.

In the case of loans against shares, account operations are equally important. Periodically, say once a fortnight, the bank would arrive at the drawing power (DP = Latest Market Value of Shares minus Margin). Should the outstanding at any point of time exceed the DP so arrived at, the borrower would be asked either to pump in additional shares to shore up the DP or to clear the excess drawing. In the worst case, the bank would sell the shares pledged and use the proceeds to bring down the excess drawing. While generally banks may decide to have such a review of DP every fortnight/ month, in case of any market meltdown, the DP review and the follow up action would not wait for fixed timelines or deadlines, it would be instantaneous.

4.3.2.3. Mortgage Loans

As is commonly understood, extension of credit against the security of an immovable property is known as "mortgage financing". Inasmuch as housing remains one of the most basic needs of individuals, mortgage financing could possibly be the most dominant loan type within the retail credit portfolio.

Once satisfied with the conditions, bank sanctions the loan, prescribing the rate of interest payable, the amount of margin money to be brought in by the borrower, schedule for release of the loan proceeds and a schedule for repayment. It also mandates that the property in question be fully insured and the insurance policy be assigned in its favour during the tenure of the loan. Also it asks the borrower to put through an equitable mortgage transaction by submitting the property documents to the bank. The loan amount is released in installments or in one go, depending upon the nature of property. The borrower is expected to repay as per the schedule specified. Should he/ she default, the bank can dispose of the property and use the proceeds for squaring off the dues in the mortgage loan account. It can also make a call on the additional security/ guarantor/ surety to get the loan dues settled.

Normally, banks have been exhibiting an extraordinary appetite for housing loans/ mortgage loans. While one of the triggers for this appetite has been the demand side surge, it is also fuelled by the fact that the default percentage is very miniscule in the case of housing loans. Add to this the regulatory concessions available for banks that extend housing loans. Besides, there is one more factor associated with housing loans. They are backed by a tangible and, more or less, easily marketable security, something that cannot be said in the case of every other type of secured loans.

4.3.2.3.1. Types of Mortgage Loan

Based on the way they are structured, mortgage loans can broadly be classified as per the diagram below:

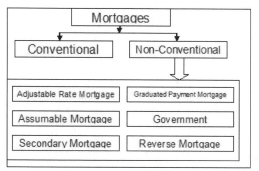

Figure 7 – Types of Mortgage

4.3.2.3.1.1. Conventional Mortgage

These are run-of-the-mill and commonplace mortgage loans. Here everything is by and large standardised. The loan amount is generally 75 — 80 per cent of the property value. Rate of Interest is fixed at the time of sanction and remains so throughout the entire tenure of the loan. Generally the borrower repays the loan by way of equated monthly installments the horizon of which may spread between 10 and 30 years. By their very nature, these are off-the-shelf loans. There is very little structuring involved in such loans.

4.3.2.3.1.2. Unconventional Mortgage

There are innumerable variants that can be collectively labeled "unconventional mortgage loans". These are different from conventional mortgage loans in their structuring. In most countries, as mortgage markets mature, more and more product variants get introduced. These vary in their design and structuring. Each one is meant to take care of certain specific requirements/ needs of the potential clients. Thus, one finds a number of unconventional mortgage loan offerings in the US and UK. In the Indian context, these are early days yet. Nonetheless, in the last couple of years, banks and housing finance companies have started offering some unconventional mortgage products to suit the needs of individual customers. The below are some of the variants of unconventional mortgage products.

4.3.2.3.1.3. Adjustable Rate Mortgage (ARM)

The name tells it all. The rate of interest payable on the mortgage is kept 'floating'. Both the bank and the customer agree upon the benchmark rate — usually a rate that is widely recognised. They also agree on the spread or mark-up above the accepted benchmark rate. Besides, how often interest rate reset would be carried is also agreed upon between the customer and bank. Under ARM, the rate payable by the borrower would vary depending upon the movement in the benchmark rate. To avoid extreme movement of interest rate under ARM, the borrower and the bank may agree upon a cap, floor or collar for the rate.

The chief advantage of an ARM is that both the bank and the borrower are not locking themselves to a fixed rate commitment for the entire duration of the loan. But the downside is, there is no predictability about the interest quantum (and as a consequence, the total repayment commitment).

4.3.2.3.1.4. Graduated Payment Mortgage (GPM)

In simple terms, graduated payment mortgage (GPM) comes with a stepped-up repayment schedule. Initial installment amounts are kept very minimum. And at periodic intervals, the installment amount is stepped up by a pre-determined factor. GPM is very much suitable for those young home buyers who are just beginning their career and who do not have high levels of disposable income, but expect to see their incomes go up in future. One unique fallout of the GPM model is that in the initial periods, the installment amount may not be adequate even to cover the interest charge. The outcome is an increase in the loan outstanding amount after every installment payment/ application of interest in the initial periods. Technically, this is called "negative amortisation"[6].

4.3.2.3.1.5. Assumable Mortgage

This is another interesting variant of mortgage financing. Here, when a house property under mortgage to an institution is sold, the buyer of the property is allowed to take over (or assume) the mortgage loan. In other words, he/ she would step into the shoes of the original owner-cum-borrower. The advantage for the buyer is that he does not have to shelve out the entire value of the house to the seller. It is enough if he/ she shells out the negotiated price of the property minus the outstanding in the seller's mortgage account. Generally for permitting such assumption of mortgage outstanding by the buyer, the mortgage lender expects to be paid a certain percentage fee.

4.3.2.3.1.6. Government Mortgage

Such a type is mostly prevalent in the US mortgage markets. In such a mortgage financing, the lender is protected by an insurance cover (for the amount outstanding) offered by some government agency. Should the borrower default, the concerned agency would step in and pay the dues to the lender.

4.3.2.3.1.7. Secondary Mortgage

This involves a property already under, mortgage. Under secondary mortgage, a second lender steps in, funds against the property already

---

[6] Amortisation is the process of wiping off the loan component

under mortgage to another lender. The second lender's rights over the property are residuary and are inferior to that of the first lender. Should the borrower default, the property would be sold and the proceeds would first be used to square off the dues to be paid to the first lender. Only after that, the balance proceeds, if any, would be made available for clearing the amount due to the second lender. Everything else remaining the same, the rate of interest on second mortgage would be higher than that on ordinary mortgage. Secondary mortgage can be used to raise money on an existing property which is already under mortgage.

4.3.2.3.1.8. Smart Mortgage

Earlier an account called "Sweep Account", which is a blend of Savings and Term Deposit accounts was discussed. Similarly some banks offer a Special Mortgage Loan – linking the home loan account with a savings account. The interest on the home loan is charged on a daily basis taking into account the balance in the Savings account (i.e. interest is charged on the difference between the balance in the home loan and the balance in the Savings Account).

4.3.2.3.1.9. Reverse Mortgage

In a sense, it is an 'atypical' mortgage transaction. Reverse mortgage is a mirror image of other normal mortgage transactions. Here, the cash flow sequences can be designed to be exactly opposite to what they would be in normal mortgage transactions. Bank lends money to an existing home owner against his/ her equity—called Home Owner's Equity (HOE) – in the house property. During the tenure of the reverse mortgage loan, ownership of the house remains with the owner. As per the market practice in the US, the borrower needs to occupy the house property against which he/ she is raising money. Reverse mortgages have the utility for those senior citizens who have a house property but do not have adequate monthly Income.

Under reverse mortgage, the mode of drawing money could be of four types: -
- Lump sum
- Monthly payment

- Line of credit
- Hybrid

Under lump sum scheme one goes by the lender to the borrower/ home owner. In the case of monthly payment scheme, reverse mortgage transaction is entered into and the borrower is paid a fixed sum every month for a certain number of years. Reverse mortgage can also be used for obtaining a line of credit. This means, the borrower is given a limit and he/ she can keep drawing the amount whenever he/ she needs money subject to the condition that at any point of time the total outstanding in the account does not exceed the limit set. In other words, in this instance, a running Overdraft (OD) account gets created on the backing of the reverse mortgage. Hybrid mode involves a combination of two or all three modes indicated above.

4.4   Retail Loan — Generic Appraisal Process

As a process, retail credit starts with the submission of loan application by the prospective borrower. Such submission can be in person, post, through direct selling agent network or, in the case of tech-savvy banks, through online. Post-submission, there is a preliminary scrutiny by the credit department which verifies the proposal *prima facie*. If the application is in order in every respect and all the necessary supporting documents are made available, then it is taken up for detailed appraisal. Appraisal is the stage where a bank looks at the proposal in detail both in the personal front of the applicant and the viability of the project applied for. In the retail segment such appraisal can either be manual or automated. However, given the fact that the number of proposals to be handled would be high, it may not be possible to have an in depth manual appraisal. To overcome this difficulty, banks may use automated appraisal mechanisms to vet and decide on individual proposals. It is entirely upto the individual banks to take a view whether they would use such an automated appraisal system as a decision making system (DMS) or a decision support system (DSS). Post-detailed appraisal, a decision is taken on the sanction or rejection of the proposal.

Business Initiation	Origination Customer Acquisition	Transaction Management	Customer Experience Management	Collection Management	Risk Management
Product Definition	Customer Acquisition	Transaction Processing	24X7 Help Desk	Delinquency Management	Risk Identification
Parameter Settings	Application Data Capture	Fund transfer	Call Centre Management	Ageing/Profile	Risk Evaluation
Products	Application Processing	Payment methods		Early Collections	Risk Management
Loans			Statement		
	Credit Scoring	Fee , Interest & Charges Posting	generations	Late Collections	Risk Control
Cash loans					
Auto loans	Behavioral Scoring			Queues based processing	Risk Analytics
Consumer Loans		Clearing	Welcome Packs		
Dealer loan	Interaction with Credit			Reminder Cycles	Fraud Detection & Control
Sales Finance	Bureaus	Standing Instructions	Promotional		
Mortgages			campaigns	Promises to Pay	
Home Improvement	Credit Limit sanctions	Authorizations			Credit Risk
			Cross sell	Payment History	
Cards	Agreement/account	Collateral	activities		Liquidity Risk
	Creation	Management		Dispute Resolutions	
		Write Off		Collector's Performance Monitoring	

Figure 8 – Generic Retail Appraisal Process

If the proposal is sanctioned, generally banks stipulate a set of conditions to be complied with by the borrower. Some of these conditions could be required to be complied with before the disbursement of the loan (pre-disbursement conditions) while there may be a few others that may be prescribed for compliance during/ after disbursement (post disbursement conditions). Generally banks ensure that all pre-disbursement conditions are satisfied by the borrower before the release of funds. Also they make sure that the borrower concerned puts through the necessary documentation before availing himself/ herself of the loan sanctioned, as any release of funds without proper documentation could endanger the bank's interests. Once the loan is disbursed, it is the responsibility of the retail credit department/ branch to ensure that all the post-disbursement conditions too are complied with by the borrower within a reasonable time. Besides, post-disbursement is a time for keeping an eagle's eye on the conduct of the account. Such monitoring is done to identify those accounts where there is a slippage in meeting the repayment commitments and to effect immediate remedial action. If and when a retail account gets into rough weather, apart from sending routine reminders to borrowers, some banks use their recovery agents to follow up and get the repayment. If default persists despite such monitoring and follow up, banks start invoking all available contractual and legal remedies for recovering their dues. While this is the generic picture of retail credit process, the details could differ from bank to bank depending upon their internal credit and recovery policies as well as their individual risk appetite/ aversion.

4.4.1. Five 'C's of the borrower

Confidence is the basis of all credit transactions. This is the cornerstone of every credit application. Lack of confidence on the prospective borrower leads to a rejection of the proposal ab-initio.

The basis of this confidence is generally derived from the **5 'C's** of the prospective borrower i.e. **character, capacity, capital, collateral** and **conditions**. In addition to the 5 C's reliability, responsibility and resources are also looked into for gaining the confidence.

4.4.1.1. Character:

Character is the paramount quality the lending Institution demands, while processing the Credit Proposal. The foundation of long term relationship with the Borrower commences with the favourable opinion formed by the Lender on the Character, Ability and Willingness of the Borrower, apart from looking into other aspects of "Background Check" or credit scoring.

The character of the borrower, which indicates his intention to repay, is very important even in contradicting situations, where the Borrower may have the ability to repay or totally unable to repay. Willingness on his/ her part will somehow ensure complete repayment of the Loan.   A questionable integrity would make every banker shun him/ her, even if backed by sufficient collaterals.

Character of a borrower is constituted by honesty, sobriety, good habits, personality, the ability and willingness to keep his word at all times and the honouring of the commitments under all circumstances.

Currently, there are means of knowing of such integrity with the Central Bank of the country publishing list of defaulter's database.

Character of the borrower can also be gauged by an interaction with him/ her. The process of interaction also discloses the genuineness of purpose in his/ her mind.

4.4.1.2. Capacity:

The Capacity of the borrower reveals his/ her ability to stand in good stead in hours of crisis both financially and psychologically.

It deals with the ability of the borrower to manage an enterprise or venture successfully with the resources available to him. His/ the management team's educational, technical and professional qualifications, antecedents/ the past track record of the enterprise, present activity, experience in the line of business, experiences of the family, special skill or knowledge possessed by him/ the collective knowledge base of the enterprise, his past record etc., would give an insight into his capacity to manage the show successfully and repay the loan.

4.4.1.3. Capital:

It is the amount to be brought in by the Borrower to stake his claim in the business i.e., borrower's margin. The owned funds concept being his/ her ability to meet the loss, if any, sustained in the Business and not solely depending on the Creditor/ Banker for the bail-out. This is also a minimum level of commitment anticipated from the Borrower by the Credit Appraisal Authorities.

However in respect of Venture Capital Funds, Innovative Ideas of the Borrowers take precedence over the Capital Infusion Arrangements.

4.4.1.4. Collateral:

Collateral means the type of security to be brought in by the Borrower, either in the form of tangible or intangible assets for securing the loan.

Tangible refers to assets in physical form, while, intangible pertains to non–physical attributes such as, reputation, brand image, Goodwill, Patents and Trademark etc. Even a third party surety/ guarantee can be treated as intangible. The Collaterals are being stipulated depending upon the background of the borrower and also the quantum of finance sought by.

The collateral comes handy to the lenders to enforce the securities, in case of default committed by the borrowers. In case of tight monetary conditions prevailing in the market, higher collaterals are stipulated by way of margin on the quantum of finance being availed by the Borrowers.

4.4.1.5. Conditions:

The terms/ conditions stipulated by the credit lending authorities for availing loans are called as 'conditions'. It may be of pre-sanction/ post-sanction in nature.

Pre-sanction formalities relate to, adherence to certain terms and conditions and completion of documentation prior to disbursal of the loan Installments /loan amount.   Post-sanction formalities relate to compliance with the terms and conditions of the loan post disbursal.
For instance pre sanction formalities of compliance with certain conditions from the statutory authorities like the Tax/ the Municipal Authorities regarding fulfilling of the statutory obligations.

The post–sanction formalities confine mainly to the upkeep of collateral in good condition satisfying the requirement of the lending authorities.

Besides this, the following qualities of a borrower also help the bank in appraising the borrower for a lending decision – Competence, Initiative, Intelligence, Drive & Energy, Self-confidence, Frankness and   Patience.

The 5Cs mentioned above are qualitative in nature and very difficult to compare with others. The below table is a suggestive nature to quantify the 5Cs of the prospective borrower (it is a only an indicative one and not a standard). The concept of Credit Scoring takes care of all these into account. In countries where Credit Scoring is not yet fully in vogue, due to various reasons like non-availability of unique Social security number, etc., this can be of use.

Table 1 – Quantification of 5Cs

#	Particulars	Excellent – 3 marks	Good – 2 marks	Poor – 1 mark
1.	Character	Honest. Keeps his words at all times.	Makes efforts to keep his words.	
2.	Personal Attention of Promoter	Fully involved and is the only source of income for the borrower.	Has other sources of income.	
3.	Competence	Has knowledge and experience in the line of activity and is assisted by able functionaries in key positions.	Has knowledge and experience in the line of activity and is assisted by professionals competent in the line of activity.	Has knowledge nor experience in the line of activity.
4.	Drive & Energy	From the front and fully involved.	Fairly energetic. Generally gets involved in all activities.	Avoid work.
5.	Transparency	Speaks out about the weaknesses in the line of activity as well as the relative weakness of his business vis-à-vis the competitors.	Prepared to speak out about the weaknesses in the line of activity as well as the relative weakness of his business vis-à-vis the competitors, but after probing.	

Retail Banking   75

#	Particulars	Excellent – 3 marks	Good – 2 marks	Poor – 1 mark
6.	Confidence	Has complete self-belief.	Believes in his abilities.	
7.	Financial Resources	Proves his financial ability to not only meet the margin requirements, but also has buffer to finance over runs, delays etc.	Has resources to fund the margin as well as meet overruns marginally.	

4.4.2. Retail Credit — Manual and Automated Appraisal

It is a topic of ongoing and never ending debate – whether Credit Appraisal is an art or science. For academic purposes, it can be viewed as a combination of art and science. If it is science it will fit into some logic and hence can completely be automated. If it is an art, no system can support it. For calculation of the ratios, profit and other figures, eligible loan amount, Credit scoring, etc., the systems can support the appraising authorities. However, in the case of 5Cs, etc., the in-person interview with the borrower can only reveal lot of ideas which can lead to lending decisions. As has been discussed above, appraisal is the process of taking a detailed view on a credit proposal and deciding whether to sanction or reject it. In the ordinary course, and it happens in wholesale banking, appraisal is better carried out manually by bank's officials. However, in the case of retail credit, this may not be feasible at all because of the sheer number of proposals that pour in. Sticking on to manual appraisal to handle huge volumes of proposals may not be cost effective either. Besides, there is one more aspect of retail credit proposals that make them more amenable to automated appraisal. That is, the kind of data that go into the appraisal process is more or less standard. Also the way retail credit loan applications are structured and information is sought, it is very much amenable for automated appraisal.

4.4.3. Borrowing: What is the differentiator?

When a borrower borrows from a bank, he/ she can do it in style. In fact, in different styles. He can ask the bank to sanction an overdraft (OD) against any acceptable security and set it up as a running account. Thus, he can draw whatever amount he wants, whenever he wants, subject to his having sufficient "drawing power". Besides, if he happens to have excess cash on a day, he can just leisurely walk to the bank branch and deposit it, thus bringing down the outstanding as well as the concomitant interest burden. Thus, life becomes simple for when in the case of OD running account.

The other case is, when a borrower has been sanctioned an OD and the bank expects him to draw the whole amount in one shot and repay the same in pre-agreed installments. In this situation, he cannot tap the OD account whenever he wants. Nor can he deposit excess cash in the account whenever he feels like.

The third type is, a borrower have been sanctioned an OD and he is asked to withdraw the whole amount in one shot, with, a condition that he needs to repay it in one go after a certain period of time. Like the previous case, this kind of facility is quite restrictive. In banking parlance, such a facility is known as 'demand loan'.

4.5 Know Your Customer (KYC) Policy

Banks have been mandated from time to time relating to proper identification of account holders mainly the borrowers and the need for compliance of extant system and procedures to help in preventing frauds, known as KYC norms.

Know Your Customer defined:

- Obtain & verify basic background information on the borrower.
- Obtain & verify evidence of regulatory clearance and registrations like CST/ST registration papers, IT PAN etc.,

Customer identification is a very important step. This can be established by verifying the evidence produced by the borrower about his identity, signature and address proof. Carrying out checks of the evidence produced by the borrower independently about his identity is must.

4.6 Non-Performing Assets (NPA)

When the repayment for a loan is regular it is a standard asset and is called Performing Asset. Else it is non-performing assets. As per the policy of income recognition the interest income for the banks should be based on record of recovery. While granting loans and advances, realistic repayment schedules may be fixed on the basis of cash flows with borrowers. An asset, including a leased asset, becomes non-performing when it ceases to generate income for the bank. A non-performing asset (NPA) is a loan or an advance where;

- Interest and/ or installment of principal remain overdue for a period of more than 90 days in respect of a term loan
- The account remains 'out of order' in respect of an Overdraft/ Cash Credit (OD/ CC)
- The bill remains overdue for a period of more than 90 days in the case of bills purchased and discounted
- A loan granted for short duration crops will be treated as NPA, if the installment of principal or interest thereon remains overdue for two crop seasons.
- A loan granted for long duration crops will be treated as NPA, if the installment of principal or interest thereon remains overdue for one crop season
- The outstanding balance remains continuously in excess of the sanctioned limit/ drawing power.
- In cases where the outstanding balance in the principal operating account is less than the sanctioned limit/ drawing power, but there are no credits continuously for 90 days as on the date of Balance Sheet or credits are not enough to cover the interest debited during the same period.

Depending on the age of the non-performance of the assets, uniform health code system indicating the quality or health of individual advances are introduced in India and depending on the health code banks need to make provisions. The similar coding system is also available in other countries.

Table 2 – NPA loans health code

Description	Health code
Satisfactory	1
Irregular	2
Stick: Viable-under nursing	3
Stick: Non-viable/ sticky	4
Advances recalled	5
Suit filed accounts	6
Decreed accounts	7
Bad and doubtful debts	8

4.7   Chapter Summary

- In the case of retail credit, banks may use either manual or automated appraisal. In either case, most banks use a framework by name `credit scoring model' for appraisal of loan proposals.

- Banks may offer retail credit facilities at fixed or floating interest rate. Similarly, banks may offer different kinds of repayment schedule to suit individual customers.
- Banks offer both unsecured and secured credit facilities to their retail customers. Secured loan could be against deposits, shares, house property, etc. Depending upon the nature of the security offered, banks establish their right over the same through pledge, hypothecation, lien, assignment or mortgage.
- Mortgage financing is ubiquitous credit facility in the retail segment. In developed markets, there are quite many variants of such financing such as adjustable rate mortgage (ARM), graduated payment mortgage (GPM), assumable mortgage, government mortgage, secondary mortgage and reverse mortgage.

*****

Chapter 5. Payment Systems

Going by the classical definition, banking is all about accepting deposits for the purpose of lending and/ or investment. But, in reality, banks do much more than accepting deposits, lending and investing. They also serve as vehicles for moving money from one person to another and from one place to another. In fact, acting as payment conduit is one of the two USPs of the very banking companies as compared with any other type of financial institutions. This USP accrues to banks primarily because of the fact that they offer chequeable accounts and are one of the direct participants in the "payment system". From a definitional angle, payment system is the mechanism using which funds move from one bank to another and thus from one person to another and also from one place to another. It is variously called "Payment System", "Payment & Settlement System", "Clearing System" or "Clearing & Settlement System". Payment System, because of what it delivers, is the backbone of any economy. In fact, in today's world, the entire economy would come to a standstill if there were no Payment System in place. The efficiency of various other economic agents in an economy is directly dependent on the efficiency of the Payment System.

5.1. Operational Mechanics

It is easier to define that inter-bank movement of funds happens through the Payment System. But how does this happen in terms of operational details? Such a question is better understood by going through an illustration.

Let us take the district town of Chennai. Say, there are only six banks in the town. And they are: ABC Bank, EDF Bank, GHI Bank, JKL Bank, MNO Bank and PQR Bank. The fundamentals of the functioning of any Payment System remain the same regardless of the number of banks/ branches involved, however it gets complicated with more banks/ branches. To get a better understanding, let us view the Payment System from the point of view of one of the six banks indicated above, say, ABC Bank.

On any day, there would be a lot of customers of ABC Bank, who would be depositing cheques drawn on any one of the other five banks in that city. Inasmuch as these cheques are not drawn on it, ABC Bank cannot obviously effect payment to its customers. It segregates all such other banks' cheques, group and bundle them bank-wise and sends to the other five banks individually, tender the bundled cheques and get equivalent cash from the respective banks. A simple solution, but it is also the most inefficient way of getting money from other banks.

Nonetheless, that was precisely the way in which funds moved in the City of London when banking was at its infancy - 1770 C.E. In fact, those staff members who would go to each and every other bank in the day to get money were branded as "walking clerks".

Here comes the clearing system handy – this system is making the representatives of all the banks congregate in one common place and exchange cheques. And the place where bank representatives congregate and carry out such an exchange is called the "clearing house". Before going to the clearing house, ABC Bank prepares a list of cheques drawn on other five banks in that centre and the aggregate amount receivable from each of them. At this stage, the bank knows only the amount of money to be received from every other bank. Then, the representative of the ABC bank goes to the clearing house carrying these 'outward' cheques. There, the bank presents the concerned cheques to the representatives of the respective banks. In return, ABC Bank receives cheques drawn on it — called "inward cheques" from all other five banks. These are cheques issued by ABC bank's customers and given to the customers of other five banks. Naturally, therefore, in these cases, ABC Bank has to make payment to those respective banks. Once this exercise is done, representative of ABC Bank would arrive at the amount of money the bank has to pay to every other bank. At this juncture, the representative quickly nets and computes the amount receivable and payable by ABC Bank *vis-à-vis* every other bank separately. This process is called "bilateral netting".

It is possible to complete the payment process at this stage, if ABC Bank were to receive or pay through individual cheques from/ to the five other banks. Such "bilateral netting" is an okay solution, but still is not the most optimal one. Hence, what ABC Bank does (as do the other five banks in) is to arithmetically aggregate the bilateral receivables/ payables with respect to other five banks and arrive at the net of all net figures. This process is called "multilateral netting". The outcome of such multilateral netting is reckoned as the amount payable/ receivable by ABC Bank with respect to the very clearing house. A similar exercise is carried out by the other five banks too. At the end of such a multilateral netting exercise, each bank would have come to know of the net amount payable/ receivable by it with respect to the clearing house. If, for an individual bank, the multilateral net amount is receivable, the clearing house credits the concerned bank's account with that amount. Conversely, when the multilateral net amount is payable by an individual bank, its account is debited by the clearing house. This is precisely the way in which inter-bank fund movement and settlement happen.

Going by the above, for a clearing system to function effectively, it is mandatory all the member banks maintain an account with one common agency. Such an agency is called the 'settlement agency' and the accounts so maintained are christened the 'settlement accounts'. In general, in most countries, it is the central bank of that country (or its representative bank) that acts as the settlement agency. In Chennai, let us suppose, MNO Bank is acting as the settlement agency. This means, all the other banks would have to necessarily maintain a Current Account with MNO Bank, Chennai. At the end of each day, MNO Bank would credit/ debit the settlement accounts of all the clearing house member banks with the amount payable to/ receivable from them. As should be obvious, in any clearing process, the aggregates of such amounts receivable from and payable to different member banks need to match on any day. This is because, as a process, clearing is a zero-sum game and the clearing house is just a routing pipeline.

Of course, the above narration carries an innocent presumption. That is that, all the cheques presented by each bank would be paid by the other banks. Reality, however, is entirely different. Cheques bounce quite frequently for various reasons. Thus, some of the cheques presented, for instance, by ABC Bank to MNO Bank may be returned unpaid by the latter.

And the same holds good vis-à-vis the cheques presented to other banks by ABC Bank. On its part, ABC Bank itself may return some of the cheques issued by its customers and received from other banks through clearing. Such cheque returns are adjusted through a separate return clearing. And the multilateral net amount payable/ receivable by each in respect of "returned cheques" is actually arrived in the same way as above, but separately. In fact, the net amount payable to/ receivable from any bank by the clearing house is actually arrived by taking into account the 'clearing' and the "return clearing" payable/ receivable figures. It is generally the net figure that is debited/ credited in the settlement accounts of individual banks.

Note: The bank presenting a cheque to the clearing house is called "Presenting Bank" or "Collecting Bank" and the bank which receives and pays the Cheque is called "Paying Bank".

This process is now more complicated with around 100 banks operating in a city each having around 100 branches. Without a computer system calculating the net amount payable/ receivable is very difficult – in fact almost impossible.

5.1.1. Payment System - Classification

It is possible to classify the Payment System into various types, using different bases/ criteria: Value of permissible transactions, extent of automation used, impact of transaction, settlement methodology and message origin.

5.1.1.1. Value of Individual Transactions

On the basis of the value of transactions permitted, payment systems can be classified as retail, large value and hybrid. As the name itself implies, retail payment systems are meant for only small value instruments. In such payment systems, individual payment/ instrument value cannot exceed a pre-set ceiling amount. For instance, in one of the payment systems in vogue in India, individual payments cannot exceed ₹5 lacs. This system is so designed that any individual payment instrument that exceeds ₹5 lacs in value would automatically be weeded out. Similarly, in the Indian context, there is also one more payment system where an individual payment instrument cannot cross ₹2 Crores. In simple terms, such payment systems are essentiality retail in their character.

Large value payment systems are the exact opposite of the above. In such payment systems, an individual payment instruction needs to be over and above a minimum threshold limit. Any payment instrument for an amount less than the said cut-off limit would not at all be entertained by the system. For instance, in the Indian context, in metros there is a payment system by name "High Value Clearing". This is meant for those instruments of value ₹1 lac and above.

Hybrid payment systems entertain both high value and very low value payments. In other words, these systems are indifferent to the amount of individual payment instruments. Incidentally, the most widespread clearing mechanism (namely, MICR clearing or normal clearing) in India is a hybrid payment system.

5.1.1.2. Extent of Automation

On the basis of extent of automation used, clearing and settlement systems can be classified as manual, totally electronic or hybrid. The clearing and settlement system that is in vogue in some of the district centres/ small towns in India is manual. In such centres, presentment, processing and settlement are manual. There is very little automation associated with it. On the other hand, in some developed countries, there are payment and settlement systems that are totally automated and that use straight through processing (STP). In such systems, end-to-end payment flow and processing happen electronically with very little human intervention. The backbone payment system in the US, namely, Fedwire is a classic example of such a totally automated payment system.

In a hybrid system, part of the processing is manual, while the balance is automated. For instance, the clearing and settlement system that is in vogue in all the metros in India as of now is hybrid.

5.1.1.3.   Message Type/ Origin

One may classify payment systems based on the type of payment instruction that can get originated in them. Most payment systems allow the sender/ bank remitting money to trigger the transaction/ instruction. And such systems are known as "credit transfer" systems. Example of such transactions would be – automatic credit of periodical interest/ dividends. But at the same time, there are also a few payment systems that allow the receiver/ beneficiary to emanate a payment transaction. These are called "debit transfer" systems. Example of such transactions would be – payment of phone bills, credit card payments, loan EMIs, etc. Needless to say, debit transfer systems are somewhat deicer, compared to "credit transfer" systems. Also there could be returns on account of non-availability of funds, etc. In most countries, the backbone payment system is a "credit transfer" system. Of course, nowadays, "debit transfer" systems also co-exist with such backbone systems, but with a lot of restrictions. Thus, in India, the back bone payment system, namely MICR clearing system, is a "credit transfer" system. At the same time, India has a restricted payment system by name "Electronic Clearing Service- Debit" or "ECS-Debit" which is an out and out "debit transfer" system alongwith "ECS-Credit".

5.1.1.4.   Transaction Impact

Payment and Settlement Systems can also be classified as "real time-and deferred" on the basis of the amount of time required for account impact of individual payment messages/ transactions. In real time payment systems, individual payment transactions are processed, communicated and money moved from the account of one bank to another bank almost-instantaneously. In other words, within seconds of the remitter remitting money in his bank, the payee's account maintained with another bank is credited. Most countries have such real time payment systems. The oldest of these is the 'Fedwire' of the US. And CHAPS, an acronym, is the UK equivalent of it. In the Indian context too real time payment systems are in place.

In the case of deferred payment/ settlement system, the actual movement of funds from one bank to another does not happen instantaneously for every payment instruction. Movement of funds between banks happens at pre-designated points of time. This necessarily means settlement is bunched in the case of deferred payment systems. By the way, the focus is on settlement or movement of funds, not on transmission of payment messages. For, even under a deferred payment system, payment messages, but not money, may flow from one bank to another instantaneously.

5.1.1.5.   Settlement Methodology

The way money flows from one bank to another differs according to the settlement methodology associated with the system. In the case of a gross settlement system, each individual bank may pay the other beneficiary bank for every payment instruction separately. In such a settlement system, one bank's payable *vis-à-vis* another bank is not netted against its relevant receivables.

On the other hand, under net settlement system, individual banks aggregate their payables and receivables and net them to arrive at "net payable" or "net receivable". If a bank carries out such netting with respect to every other bank individually in the system, then that is called "bilateral netting". Instead, if each bank nets its receivables and payables *vis-à-vis* the entire universe of banks in the system, such a netting exercise is called "multilateral netting". Of the two types of netting discussed above, from a systemic angle, multilateral netting is a more efficient mechanism to employ.

5.1.2.   Payment System Types - A Combination Matrix

If one were to take a two-dimensional view of the settlement system, reckoning the time and the grossing/ netting dimensions, there arise four combinations. They are:

➢   Real Time Gross Settlement (RTGS)
➢   Real Time Net Settlement
➢   Deferred Gross Settlement (DGS)

    ➤ Deferred Net Systems (DNS)

However, of these four above, Real Time Net Settlement System is an absolute impossibility inasmuch as in real time there is no question of netting two or more transactions. In general, most payment and settlement systems adopt deferred net settlement mechanism. Also real time gross settlement (RTGS) system is in vogue in most of the countries.

5.2. Stakeholders in any Payment System

In addition to drawer, drawee, payee, negotiator, etc., who were discussed earlier the main stakeholders in any payment system are:

- Presenting Bank or Collecting Bank – who presents the instrument to other bank for payment through clearing house.
- Paying Bank – the bank on whom the instrument is drawn.
- Settlement Agency/ Clearing House – the agency who acts as mediator between all the banks in settling the payment between them.

5.3. Payment System/ Clearing & Settlement in India

Given the vast network of banks/ branches, clearing and settlement system is almost all-pervasive. In India, as per the latest reports, there are more than 1200 centres having independent clearing houses. Of course, not all of these are run by the central bank. In fact, barring a handful (in metros and some of the State headquarters), all other clearing houses are run by other commercial banks. While the overall regulations are by and large similar across centres, individual clearing houses are entitled to have their operational rules as agreed upon by their member banks. As for the major types of clearing, one can talk of the following:

5.3.1. Normal/ MICR Clearing

Of these, Normal/ MICR clearing, handles presentation of all and sundry instruments. There is no restriction as to the maximum/ threshold amount of every instrument. Cheque processing is automated in most of the centres. In terms of volume, not value, this clearing tops the list. In every centre, such normal/ MICR clearing is open to all branches of banks that are members of the clearing house. The period taken for credit of instrument proceeds would vary from centre to centre. In general, in small towns, proceeds are credited on the same working day. But in a metro city like Chennai, a customer depositing an MICR cheque, say, on Monday would get the proceeds credited to his account on Tuesday and he/ she can draw the funds only on Wednesday.

5.3.2. High Value Clearing

Unlike normal/ MICR clearing, high value clearing is restricted in its scope. In the first place, only individual instruments of value ₹1 lac and above can be presented. Besides, this clearing is available at present only in select centres. Moreover, even in such centres, not all the bank branches would be eligible to participate in high value clearing. One unique feature of this clearing is that the cheque proceeds are credited to the customers' accounts on the very date of deposit/ presentation.

5.3.3. Return Clearing

Earlier the concept of "cheque return" in clearing system was discussed. This clearing is exclusively for return of instruments presented earlier. In centres where both normal/ MICR and high value clearing systems are in place, there would be one return clearing for normal/ MICR instruments and another for high value instruments. Only after the related return clearing is complete, any settlement of funds will be effected.

5.3.4. ECS Clearing

Basically meant for mass payments, it has two variants: ECS-Credit and ECS-Debit. ECS-Credit is useful when, for instance, a corporate wants to pay interest to thousands of its depositors. By using ECS-Credit, the corporate can authorize its bank — named sponsor bank — to debit its account with the aggregate amount of such interest payments and pass on the money through Clearing House to the bank branches of its individual depositors so that these branches can credit the respective depositors' accounts. In simple terms, an ECS-Credit transaction calls for one account to be debited and multiple accounts to be credited across bank branches. The maximum amount that can be credited to a single account under ECS-Credit is ₹5 lacs.

ECS-Debit is, in a sense, a mirror image of ECS-Credit. It is useful when a public utility such as the telecom service providers want to collect telephone charges from thousands of subscribers. By making use of ECS-Debit, they can ask its bank — again, sponsor bank — to pass on through the clearing house details of amounts to be debited from the accounts of individual subscribers spread over different bank branches and get the aggregate collection credited to its account. An unbundling of ECS-Debit transaction would show that it involves debiting multiple accounts across bank branches and crediting one account. Incidentally, the quantum of amount to be debited from a single account on account of a specific ECS-Debit transaction cannot exceed a specified amount say ₹5 lacs. It goes without saying that ECS-Credit and ECS-Debit are possible only in the banks/ branches who have implemented core banking system.

5.3.5. EFT Clearing

In the first place, EFT here stands for Electronic Fund Transfer. This clearing facility is available for those banks that have offered themselves for it. At present, banks in select centres are participating in the EFT clearing. Under the EFT facility, funds can be remitted from one branch (of any of the member banks) to another branch (again of any of the member banks) situated in those centres. The actual message flow and fund flow take place through clearing house accounts of member banks. As per the extant practice, any remittance made using EFT is credited to the beneficiary's account on the same day/ very next working day. EFT suffers from a restriction that an Individual remittance amount cannot exceed a limit say ₹2 lacs. The amount is still less when the EFT request is made through Internet Banking. This is a sort of risk mitigation, since once a request is made through EFT; it cannot be withdrawn by anyone.

5.3.6.   Real Time Gross Settlement

In the Indian context, the payment system landscape has undergone a dramatic transformation with the Introduction of RTGS in early 00s. The version has been designed to enable instantaneous and irrevocable movement of funds between banks. The Indian RTGS – it has no brand name or acronym as yet – would be the country's backbone payment system – with the net payable and receivable positions of individual member banks arising – out of all other clearing and payment systems – getting settled through it.

5.3.7.   Cheque Truncation

Cheque Truncation System (CTS) or Image-based Clearing System (ICS), in India, is basically an online image-based cheque clearing system where cheque images and Magnetic Ink Character Recognition (MICR) data are captured at the collecting bank branch and transmitted electronically. In the US such a clearing system is implemented by an Act called "Check 21 Act" and hence this system itself is called as Check 21 system.

Truncation means, stopping the flow of the physical cheques issued by a drawer bank/ branch to the drawee bank/ branch. The physical instrument is truncated at some point en-route to the drawee branch and an electronic image of the cheque is sent to the drawee branch along with the relevant information like the MICR fields, date of presentation, presenting banks etc.

Cheque truncation would eliminate the need to move the physical instruments across branches, except in exceptional circumstances. This would result in effective reduction in the time required for payment of cheques, the associated cost of transit and delays in processing, etc., thus speeding up the process of collection or realisation of cheques.

While this method is in vogue in most of the countries, in India, it is being introduced in different centres one by one. The major difference here is the original instrument will be with the presenting bank and **not** with the paying bank.

5.4. Payment System - A Globetrot

When the fundamental principle of clearing remains the same across the global banking system, the operating methods may vary a little here and there. Let us have a bird's eye view of different major clearing systems of various countries.

5.4.1. United States

In the US, besides cheque payment system, there are three other payment systems in vogue: Fedwire, CHIPS and ACH. Of these, Fedwire is a real time gross settlement system and is the backbone payment system in the US.

5.4.1.1. Fedwire

Fedwire, a-quick name for Federal Wire Service, is the backbone RTGS in the US. In fact, it is used for payment by one bank to another within US. Besides, in respect of all other clearing arrangements, the net settlement funds are transferred to/ from individual banks' accounts through the Fedwire at designated points of time.

5.4.1.2. CHIPS

An acronym for **C**learing **H**ouse for **I**nter-Bank **P**ayment **S**ystem, CHIPS is used by US banks in respect of incoming remittances to the US from abroad. Unlike Fedwire, CHIPS is not an RTGS, though in effect it seems to mimic one. In reality it is a deferred net settlement system (DNS).

A large number of payment transactions are put through the CHIPS during the day by all member banks. At the end of the day (EoD), at a pre-designated point of time, CHIPS aggregates all the payments sent and received by individual member banks and arrives at the net amount payable/receivable by individual member banks by using the multilateral netting mechanism. Such net figures are communicated to individual member banks and, after a time lag of an hour or so, the same are passed on to the Federal Reserve for debit/ credit in the settlement accounts of respective member banks. Thus, unlike Fedwire, CHIPS carries out aggregated and deterred net settlement of payment transactions.

5.4.1.3. Automated Clearing Houses (ACHs)

Besides, Fedwire and CHIPS, there are also a large number of automated clearing houses (ACHs) in the US. These handle regional level automated payments and at the end of each day at a designated point of time feed the details of net payable/ receivable by member banks to Federal Reserve for onward debit/ credit of the respective settlement accounts.

In addition, of course, as is the case in other countries, in the US too there is cheque clearing centres/ houses that handle paper-based payment instruments in a small way.

5.4.2. United Kingdom

As is the case with the US and in other countries as well, in the UK, there are multiple payment and settlement systems. Besides, the Cheque and Credit Clearing (CCC) System, there is an RTGS in place by name CHAPS. Besides, BACS is a mass payment mechanism available in the UK.

5.4.2.1. CHAPS

An acronym for **C**learing **H**ouse **A**utomated **P**ayment **S**ystem, CHAPS is the UK's backbone payment system, similar in operational style to the FEDWIRE in US. It is an RTGS system that has been in place for decades. And is used for secure and instant transmission of funds by banks in the UK.

CHAPS differs from Fedwire on two counts. Unlike Fedwire, which is run by the Federal Reserve itself, CHAPS is managed by an independent entity. Only its settlement function is taken care of by the Bank of England. Besides, unlike Fedwire, CHAPS is not homogeneous. It has two variants:

CHAPS — Sterling and CHAPS —Euro. The first one is meant for transmission of Pound Sterling funds between banks within the UK. On the other hand, CHAPS — Euro is to be used for payments in Euro.

5.4.2.2. Bankers' Automated Clearing System (BACS)

BACS is a mass payment system in vogue in the UK. It is similar to ECS in India – nay, in fact, it is the other way around. Under BACS, there are three types of payments possible: Direct Credit, Direct Debit and Standing Order. Direct Credit is like Indian ECS-Credit where one party's account is debited and accounts of thousands of depositors/ investors/ employees are credited across banks. Ideal for interest, dividend and salary payments. Beneficiaries can maintain their accounts with any of the member banks/ branches. There is no restriction on that front. Direct Credit brings down the transaction cost associated with periodic mass payments by corporate. Direct Debit, on the other hand, is an equivalent of, Indian ECS Debit, where multiple accounts are debited and one corporate account is credited. Useful for public utilities such as telephone companies, power supply corporations, etc., for collection of periodic bill amounts from their subscribers.

In addition to Direct Credit and Direct Debit, BACS also offers Standing Order facility for the customers. Using this, an individual customer can pass on money from his/ her account to the account of anyone else maintained with any other bank branch in the UK. This is exactly the same as EFT in India.

5.4.3.   Japan

Like the US, Japan too boasts of four types of payment and settlement systems. There is a dedicated Bill and Cheque Clearing System to take care of paper-based instruments. There is another payment system by name Zengin, which is a nationwide mass payment system. [In this sense, it is an improved and centralised version of ECS]. Besides, in Japan there is a dedicated payment and settlement system for foreign currency transactions and it is known as 'Gaitame' or 'FCYCS', an acronym for Foreign Currency Yen Clearing System. Of course, as a developed economy, since later 1980s, Japan has in place a robust RTGS system by name BoJ-Net, a shortened version of **B**ank **of J**apan Financial **Net**work. BoJ-Net is the backbone payment system and is similar to Fedwire in every respect.

5.4.4. Unique Payment Systems

Some of the payment systems unique of its kind in the global banking are discussed below.

5.4.4.1. Large Value Transfer System — Canada

Among the many high value payment systems in the world, the Large Value Transfer System (LVTS) that is functioning in Canada is unique in some respects. Put in place during late90s, the Canadian LVTS has two segments (otherwise called tranches):

- ➢ Tranche 1 - mimics an RTGS system
- ➢ Tranche 2 - DNS (deferred net settlement) system

In other words, the same payment system can function as an RTGS or a DNS system. In analogical terms, one should say, LVTS combines both Fedwire and CHIPS.

What makes the Canadian LVTS all the more unique is the fact that every member bank can exercise the option on a day-today basis as to whether it would like to use the LVTS to function as an RTGS or a deferred net settlement system with respect to each and every other member bank severally. In other words, on the same day, Bank A can decide that LVTS would function as an RTGS with respect to Bank B, while it would function as a net settlement system with respect to Bank C. In an ideal situation, Bank A would like the LVTS to function as an RTGS with respect to riskier banks, while as a DNS *vis-à-vis* less risky banks. Again on the very next day, Bank A can change its preferences. Regardless of the choices exercised by individual banks, in respect of Tranche 2, the settlement accounts of individual member banks would be credited/ debited at the end of the day with the respective receivables/ payables.

5.4.4.2. TARGET — Pan European

An acronym for **T**rans-European **A**utomated **R**eal **T**ime **G**ross Settlement **E**xpress **T**ransfer. TARGET is a Pan-European payment system that can be used by banks and financial institutions for transmission of payment messages as well as funds from one country to another. Strictly speaking, TARGET is not an independent payment system by itself. In fact, it is only an interlink between the payment systems of different member countries.

Operationally speaking, let us suppose Jacques Chirac, a customer of Banque National de Paris (BNP) wants to remit a sum of Euro 10 million to Helmet Kohl who maintains his Account with Commerz Bank, Frankfurt. BNP uses the RTGS network of France to transmit the message. On receipt of the message, Bank of France debits the settlement account of BNP maintained with it and then passes on the message to TARGET, which functions as the interlinking system. On receipt of payment message from Bank of France, TARGET transmits the details to Bundesbank, which is the central bank of the recipient country, namely, Germany. In turn, Bundesbank transmits the message details to Commerz Bank and simultaneously credits the latter's settlement account with Euro 10 million. On its part, Commerz Bank would credit Helmet Kohl's account immediately on receipt of intimation from Bundesbank. Thus, TARGET is meant to ease real time cross-country payments within the Euro zone.

5.4.4.3. SEPA

Single Euro Payments Area (SEPA) was introduced in later 00s and still it is being evolved. All payments in euros within European Union are regarded as domestic payments even in Cross-Border junctions. They are not distinguished from the domestic payments.

5.4.4.4. SWIFT

No discussion on payment system is complete without talking about SWIFT. The acronym SWIFT stands for **S**ociety for **W**orldwide **I**nterbank **F**inancial **T**elecommunication. SWIFT is per-se is not a payment system. As the very name suggests it is a message transmission system. SWIFT allows member financial institutions worldwide to electronically exchange information amongst each other. Messages are transmitted globally through high speed communication channels on standardised message formats for many international banking operations.

SWIFT in itself is not a payment system. However, any inter-nation payment instruction is routed through SWIFT. The payment system of the originating and responding countries will be used as they are. The payment instruction is routed through SWIFT.

Hence, based on the volume of transactions both number and value, routed through SWIFT on a daily basis, SWIFT can very well be treated as a payment system.

5.5. Chapter - SUMMARY

➤ Payment System is the backbone of any economy. It is a mechanism that enables movement of funds from person to person and from place to place.

➤ Clearing is the mechanism through which funds move from bank to bank in every nook and corner of the country. And in terms of operational details, it is a simple and straightforward mechanism. Banks congregate in one place, exchange cheques drawn on each other, reckon cheque returns and arrive at the net payable/ receivable amount with respect to the entire system. Such net payable and receivable amounts are debited in the settlement account of the bank functioning as the Settlement Agency.

➤ One can classify the entire universe of payment systems using criteria such as the permissible amount of individual payment, instruments, extent of automation, settlement impact, time required for settlement, message flow pattern, etc.

➢ Taking a two dimensional view of payment systems, one can classify them as Deferred Gross Settlement System, Deferred Net Settlement System and Real Time Gross Settlement System.

➢ In India, following are the major types of clearing: Normal/ MICR Clearing, High Value Clearing, Return Clearing, ECS Clearing, EFT clearing and RTGS.

➢ In the US, the major payment systems are Fedwire, CHIPS and ACH. Of the three, Fedwire is the backbone RTGS. CHIPS is used for international payments, while ACH is for mass payment transactions. Similarly, UK has CHAPS as its backbone RTGS payment system, while BACS is the country's mass payment system. In the case of Japan, apart from the normal Bill and Cheque Clearing System, there is Zengin to take care of mass payments, while BOJ-Net is the country's backbone RTGS. Canada has a unique payment system by name LVTS, which gives a lot of operational leeway to its participant member banks. In Europe, TARGET is the cross country interlinking RTGS that enables real time movement of funds from one country to another in the Euro Zone.

➢ SEPA is an upcoming clearing system in Europe among all the Euro currency using countries – a clearing system in a single currency Euro.

➢ SWIFT is the communication channel through which payment instructions from one nation to the other are being communicated.

*****

Chapter 6. Cards

Cards are too common now to call for any introduction. Plastic money is the jargon with which they are affectionately called. Functionally speaking, cards are equivalent to currency inasmuch as they accord purchasing power. As currency does, cards also prove to be a store of value and medium of exchange. But they outsmart currency in many respects.

6.1. Background

The card has been in existence for many years. It started in the form of a card embossed with details of the cardholder (account number, name, expiration date, etc.), which could be used at a point of sale (PoS) to purchase goods or services. The magnetic stripe was soon introduced as a means of holding more data than was possible by embossing alone. The magnetic stripe also allowed cardholder details to be read electronically in a suitable terminal so that checks could be made with little or no human intervention about the balance limit of the cardholder or whether the card had been reported lost or stolen, etc.

Card technology has advanced over the years to keep ahead of the worldwide increase in card related crimes. As the criminal fraternity found ways of producing sufficiently good counterfeit cards, so also the card companies continue to introduce new ways of combating the problem. A succession of anti-fraud measures have been introduced over the years such as the hologram, the Card Verification Value (CVV, a value stored on the magnetic stripe which can be used to determine if a card has been produced illicitly), and in some cases, photographs of the cardholder.

Magnetic stripe cards have now been developed to the point where there is little or no further scope for introducing more anti-crime measures. This has caused the card associations to look at new technologies to take the plastic card into the new millennium.

One type of card which offers many benefits is the smart card; essentially a small computer chip, which has the ability to have more than one payment application resident on the card. For example a card could contain an "electronic purse" or simply e-purse to provide the equivalent of cash, usually for lower value transactions such as parking, toll payments, tickets, newspapers, etc.

In the future there may be the possibility of storing personal details such as driving license and medical records on the card.

There are many issues to be resolved before such all-embracing cards become common place, the most obvious ones being who owns the card and who controls which applications can be loaded or deleted. Today, the banks are interested mainly in providing payment related services to their customers and most of the current activity surrounds the provision of smart card based credit/ debit services sometimes with an additional electronic purse facility.

6.2. Types of Cards

Cards come with different features. Based on such features, it is possible to classify them into many distinct breeds. Some of these are well entrenched and widely known, while there are others that are fast catching up with their older cousins. In fact, one new variant —called smart card — could as well be the card of the future.

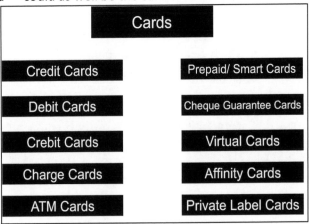

Figure 9 – Types of cards

6.2.1. Credit Card

Possibly, credit card is the most well-known species within the card family. In fact, in laymen language, card means credit card. There are two unique features which every such credit card comes embedded with; Revolving credit and the facility to pay the outstanding in deferred due date/ installments. Sure, the minimum periodic payment requirements could vary from issuer to issuer and from card type to card type. It can be 5 per cent in some cases, while 10 per cent or so in others. But that is just a difference in operational detail, not in the essence. Similarly, individual banks may keep adding feature after feature to their credit cards (insurance/ incentives/ add-ons/ no annual fee). But, in reality, these are peripherals. The core is – Revolving credit and Installment payment. Even among the merchant community, credit cards are the most well-known. In fact, at least in the Indian context, card means credit card to merchants. In countries such as the US, a credit cardholder is deemed a better credit risk than the holders of other types of cards, with the exception of charge card holders.

6.2.2. Debit Card

A comparative late entrant, internationally, debit card made its debut in the 1970s. Took time to pick up, but now is being issued by almost all the banks. The basic feature of the card is that it entitles the cardholder to use whatever balance that is available in his/ her checking/ savings account for payment transactions. In this case, the card issuer does not carry any credit risk whatsoever inasmuch as there is no extension of credit involved. Every time a cardholder uses his/ her debit card, he/ she is just drawing from distance money from his/ her account. That is it. Debit card is, thus, more of a convenience card. It can also be used to withdraw money from ATM. In certain countries as well as in the finance literature, debit card is referred to as **EFTPOS,** an acronym for Electronic Funds Transfer at the Point of Sale. Within debit cards also, there are two variants: On-line and Off-line cards. In the case of on-line cards, funds are debited instantly from the cardholder's account. Unlike on-line debit cards, off-line cards do not require the usage of PIN by the cardholder at the point of sale.

6.2.3.   Credit/ Debit Cards

Reports also speak of there being cards that can be used for a transaction either as a debit or credit card as desired by the cardholder. The choice can be exercised at the instant of payment to the merchant. Such a hybrid breed is correctly, but crazily, christened "Credit Card" or "Debit Card". Of course, Credit or Debit Cards can be used only for electronic payments through swiping machines.

Generally, it may be advantageous for card holders to avoid using debit cards for high value purchases, such as TV, Refrigerator, etc. Instead, while affecting such purchases, it is better to use one's credit card. If the purchaser has no credit card, but only a debit card, then one is better off drawing cash from the nearest ATM terminal using his/ her debit card and paying it outright. That would work out to be much cheaper for the card holder in every respect.

6.2.4.   Charge Card

Credit card comes with revolving credit and deferred payment. Charge card has a revolving time, mandates the cardholder to pay the entire card outstanding in the account, on receipt of periodic statement. In other words charge cards do not accord any credit period for the users.

Both in the Indian and international contexts, Diners charge card was the first formal card to emerge, (incidentally Diners, now coming under the Citi umbrella, continues to be a charge card). Credit cards came later on. Compared to credit cards, charge cards generally entitle a much higher spending limit for the card holders. Besides, the annual fee – in whatever name called – payable in the case of charge cards is much higher than what it is for credit cards. Generally, charge cards are issued only to premium clients.

6.2.5. ATM Card

ATM card is meant solely for transacting at ATM terminals. If a card is issued as a dedicated ATM card, it cannot be used for any other purpose. Nevertheless it can only be used in the ATMs of the concerned bank and in the other banks' ATMs. Nonetheless, such dedicated ATM cards are a vanishing species. For, nowadays, banks find it advisable to issue debit cards that can also double up as ATM cards. More details about ATM card payment process, settlement, exotic cards, etc., are discussed later in this chapter.

6.2.6. Prepaid Cards

This is a card whose magnetic strip has certain preloaded value. Each time the card is used, the stored value gets reduced by the transaction amount. Such a card is also called stored value card. In some cases prepaid card does not come with any facility for reloading. This makes it a use-and-throw item. Prepaid cards are nowadays widely used. For instance, Phone Cards, Petro Cards and Fare Cards (used in Metro trains, toll payments, etc.) are nothing but prepaid cards. Given the fact that anyone having the card can use it, prepaid cards are bearer cards. Once lost, the value therein is lost forever for the original owner.

6.2.7. Smart Card

This is nothing but a plastic card that contains an embedded microprocessor designed to store and process information. In a sense, prepaid cards discussed above are primitive ancestors to smart cards as apes are to men. Besides processing power, smart cards have many times the memory capacity of prepaid cards — ranging from 1k to 64k. However, the main distinction of a smart card over a prepaid card is the convenience of the value reloading which the former offers. In fact, it is this value reloadability feature of smart cards that has the potential to usher in a cashless society. From the users' point of view, smart cards are preferable to prepaid cards inasmuch as unauthorised usage of the former could be made difficult through application of biometrics/ password protection.

A perspective that should not be lost sight of while talking about smart cards is the fact that they are not just substitutes for credit cards or debit cards. They are much, much more. In fact, they could become repository of all information about an individual. Besides, they can also serve as identity cards and archive all transactions conducted by individuals. In other words, smart cards have a lot of applications that are waiting to be tapped. In a sense, thus, in future, smart cards would be the all-in-one cards. They would surely have Omni-presence and, possibly, omnipotence too.

6.2.8. Check Guarantee Card

This is a unique kind of card inasmuch as it essentially entitles the holder to encash cheques or pay through cheques at merchant establishments. The operational mechanism behind this card is pretty simple and, in a sense, primitive too. The cardholder is given a card that carries his/ her signature and possibly even his/ her photograph. In a way, thus, cheque guarantee card functions as an identity card. Hence, as long as any merchant establishment accepts a cheque from a check guarantee cardholder in accordance with the terms indicated on the reverse of the card, it can be assured of payment by the drawee bank. From the issuer's point of view, check guarantee card is similar to credit card in the matter of credit risk.

Reports say that check guarantee cards used to be popular in certain pockets in the US. In fact, in the Indian context, check guarantee cards were introduced as early as in the mid-1980s. If one's memory serves right, even the cheque leaves issued for, use by check guarantee cardholders used to be of fixed value. It is a different matter that check guarantee cards have failed to carve a niche for themselves in the Indian market. But that has not prevented some banks, from coming out with a card —branded Convenience Cheques— coupling the features of credit card as well as check guarantee card.

6.2.9. Virtual Card

This refers to a 'cardless' card being issued by banks nowadays. A virtual card is meant only for net payment transactions. In fact, they cannot be used by the card holder in merchant outlets inasmuch as there is no physical card at all. Internationally, banks are encouraging this as a payment mechanism for internet based transactions. Even those individuals who may have a debit/ credit card are better advised to opt for a virtual card inasmuch as the latter generally comes with a lower credit limit. Having such a lower credit limit would act as an automatic cap on the potential for frauds through the net. Moreover, those having virtual cards need not have to use or disclose their credit/ debit card numbers to any web-merchant. To that extent the potential threat of hackers and web-users misusing one's credit card or debit card gets eliminated.

6.2.10. Private Label Cards

These are dedicated cards issued primarily by establishments such as major retail chains dealing in those commodities/ products that call for repeat purchase. Such cards can be used only in the outlets run by such establishments. From the issuer's point of view, by issuing a private label card, it is able to ensure continued patronage by its customers. On the other hand, for the customer, acquiring a private label card enables him/ her to enjoy credit for his/ her purchases.

Occasionally, a bank may undertake to issue private label cards on behalf of one particular retailer/ dealer. In such cases, while the usage of the card is restricted to the specific retailer outlets, the decision to issue a card is that of the bank. In other words, in such instances, the credit risk would be that of the bank, not of the retailer.

6.2.11. Affinity Cards/ Co-branded cards

These are co-branded cards and are designed to attract people having special loyalty/ affinity for an entity/ organisation. For instance, some banks in India have in their inventory an affinity card co-branded with railway ticket booking. Here the idea is that those who have an affinity for railways would go for this card, among others.

It is easy to get confused between Private Label Cards and Affinity Cards. Hence the distinction needs to be stressed. Private Label Cards can be used only in those outlets of the tied-up retailer. On the other hand, there is no such 'outlet' restriction as far as the usage of affinity cards are concerned.

6.3. Parties associated with Credit Cards

There are primarily five players associated with any generic credit card viz.:

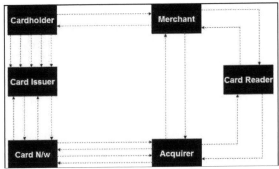

Figure 10 – Players in a card transaction

Cardholder is the one who gets the card issued in his/ her name. Issuer is that institution — generally a bank — which issues the card. In fact, the card would dominantly carry the name of the Issuer. Acquirer is an institution that acquires merchants so that they agree to accept cards of a particular affiliation like VISA or MasterCard. Merchants are those who get acquired by the acquiring institution. Card network is the entity to which the card issuer is affiliated. In fact, it is the network through which all transactions put through using the card would get settled.

Now let us take an illustration to understand the parties better. Suppose John gets a VISA Card Issued by Citibank. In this case, John is the cardholder; Citibank is the issuer while VISA is the card network. Let us presume John uses the card at Taj Hotel. Incidentally, Taj Hotel banks with Amex Bank and it is the latter that has acquired Taj Hotel into the card acceptance business. In this case, Taj Hotel is the merchant establishment, while Amex Bank is the acquirer (otherwise called acquiring bank).

In some cases, the same institution/ bank could be both the issuer and the acquirer. In the above example, suppose Citibank itself had acquired Taj Hotel, then when John uses his Citi VISA Card at the hotel, Citibank happens to be the issuer, as well as the acquirer. Occasionally, banks may also issue cards without seeking the affiliation of VISA or MasterCard. Needless to say such cards would have very limited acceptability/ reach.

6.4. Cards: Transaction Flow

When one uses his/ her credit card at a merchant establishment, apparently it all seems pretty simple— show the card, sign the slip, and walk out with the merchandise. But the fact is, every time a card gets used, series of transactions, as listed below, gets triggered.

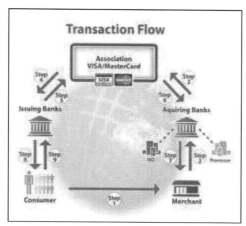

Figure 11 – A card transaction flow

1. Customer tenders his/ her card to the merchant

2. Merchant swipes the card in the card reader, enters the invoice amount through the terminal.

3. Card reader reads the info stored in the card's magnetic strip, adds details about the merchant as well as the invoice amount and passes on the message to the acquirer's processor.

4. Acquirer's processor checks the data received, forwards the same to the related card network (VISA/ MasterCard)

5. In turn the card network passes on the transaction details to the Card Issuer's processor.

6. Card Issuer verifies the credit availability, authorizes the transaction, assigns a transaction number and forwards the authorisation details to the Card Network.

7. Card Network in turn passes on the transaction authorisation details to the acquirer.

8. Acquirer's processor forwards the authorisation details to the merchant through his/ her terminal/ card reader.

9.   Merchant's terminal prints a receipt in proof of the transaction.

10. Merchant hands over the receipt as well as a copy of the invoice to the customer alongwith the merchandise. Gets the cardholder's signature in one copy and retains it as evidence.

11. At the end of the day, merchant submits to the acquirer a claim for payments due to him/ her in respect of all transactions put through during the day alongwith the copy of the signed receipt of cardholder.

12. Acquirer in turn claims the amount from the issuer through the card network.

13. Card network computes the amount payable by each card issuer in the network and passes on the net payable/ receivable details to the settlement agency.

14. Card issuer's account is debited.

15. Acquirer's account is credited.

16. Acquirer in turn credits the amount to the merchant's account.

17. Cardholder pays the outstanding in the card account according to the terms of the contract.

For better understanding of the transaction flow, let us as before suppose, John holds a VISA Card issued by Citibank, uses the card to pay Taj Hotel. Incidentally, Taj Hotel is banking with and has been acquired by Amex Bank. Against this backdrop, the **transaction flow** would be as under:

A. John tenders his card to Taj Hotel.

B. Taj Hotel staff member swipes the card in the card reader, enters the invoice amount through the terminal.

C. Card reader reads the info stored in the card's magnetic strip, adds details about Taj Hotel as well as the invoice amount and passes on the message to Amex Bank's processor.

D. Amex Bank's processor checks the data received, forwards the same to the VISA network.

E. In turn, the VISA Network passes on the transaction details to Citibank's processor.

F. Citibank verifies the credit availability, authorizes the transaction, assigns a transaction number and forwards the authorisation details to the VISA Network

G. VISA Network In turn passes on the transaction Cards: Transaction Flow authorisation details to Amex Bank's processor.

H. Amex Bank's processor in turn passes on the authorisation details to Taj Hotel through the terminal/ card reader.

I. Taj Hotel's terminal prints a receipt in proof of the transaction.

J. Taj Hotel hands over the receipt as well as a copy of the invoice to John.

K. At the end of the day, Taj Hotel submits to Amex Bank a claim for payments due to it in respect of all transactions put through during the day.

L. Amex Bank in turn claims the amount from Citibank through the VISA Network.

M. VISA Network computes the amount payable by each card issuer in the network and passes on the net-net payable/ receivable details to the settlement agency.

N. Citibank's account is debited and the Amex Bank's account is credited by the settlement agency.

O. Amex Bank in turn credits Taj Hotel's account.

P. Citibank debits the amount to the card holder's account.

Q. John pays the outstanding in the card account according to the terms of the contract.

6.4.1. Card Transactions: Settlement

While it is acceptable to talk about transaction flow *vis-à-vis* individual credit card transactions, in most countries settlement of credit card transactions (and for that matter most other inter-bank transactions) among banks happens, taking into account the entire basket of transactions occurring during a designated time bucket (say, a day).

For the purpose of our understanding, let us suppose there is a closed system with just two banks, viz., ABC Bank and XYZ Bank. Both the banks issue VISA credit cards. And both have acquired a good number of merchants. Given this, on any day, it is possible; there would be a number of ABC Bank's VISA cardholders who would be using their cards at a good number of merchant outlets acquired by XYZ Bank. While such merchant outlets would have to be paid by XYZ Bank, the latter has to get reimbursement from ABC Bank, the card issuer. Similarly, on the same day, a number of XYZ Bank's VISA cardholders would be using their cards at merchant outlets acquired by ABC Bank. In such cases, ABC Bank is duty bound to pay its merchants, while it has to seek reimbursement of the amount so paid from XYZ Bank, the card issuer.

The card network gets details of reimbursement due from one bank to another and nets off the same. Thus, card network would arrive at the net amount payable/ receivable by ABC Bank and XYZ Bank. Let us suppose, on that day the net position is in favour of XYZ Bank, i.e., the amount to be reimbursed by ABC Bank to XYZ Bank is more than what the latter needs to reimburse to the former. Having arrived at the net payable/ receivable position, the card network would pass on the message to the settlement agency (Central Bank or any other bank) indicating that ABC Bank's account (maintained with Central bank/ settlement bank) is debited with the net payable amount and XYZ Bank's account be credited. Central Bank/ settlement Bank gives effect to such debit/ credit instructions at the time of inter-bank clearing. What appears above is a simplified version. For, in reality, there are not just two banks; there are umpteen of them in the system. Under such a situation, the netting could be multilateral, not just bilateral as illustrated below.

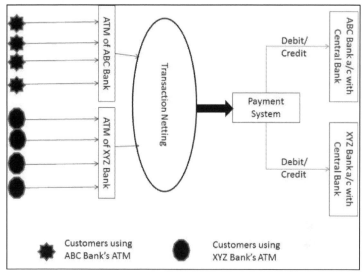

Figure 12 – Card Settlement Process

6.5. ATM Cards

Of all the inventions and innovations associated with banking during the 20th century, Automated Teller Machine (ATM) stands out (literally too). This is because; it is one invention that has changed the very face of banking, again both literally and figuratively. It has made 'branching' easier and cheaper and thus has enabled the spread of banking to every nook and corner. Today, ATM's ubiquity is the cause as well as the effect of its influence. In more than one sense, as a delivery channel, ATM is without parallel. One can say so at least till such time net banking cannibalizes it. If at all, that is.

6.5.1. ATMs - Possible Functionalities

When they came on the scene first, Cash Dispensers could no more than spit out cash. Today, the functionality of ATMs is wide. Some of them are listed below:

Table 3 – Functionalities of an ATM

Balance Enquiry	Investment Advice
Statement of Accounts	Mutual Fund Investment
Cash Withdrawal	Insurance Selling
Cash Deposit	Electronic Purse Loading
Cheque Cashing	Ticketing
Cheque Deposit	Airlines – check in
Funds transfer	Map printing
Bill Payment	Cheque book request
Currency Exchange	Stop Cheque Instruction
Loan Application	Stop Cheque revocation
Vending of merchandise	

Most of the functionalities indicated above, are self-explanatory. However, a few in the list could sound high flying. Cheque cashing, for instance. There are ATMs, which can tender a cheque and draw cash. Similarly, certain ATMs can handle multiple currencies and thus can exchange one country's currency for the other. There are also ATMs that can accept request for credit (loan application). Similarly, ATMs which use a bit of artificial intelligence can also offer investment advice. Of course, ATMs are also used for product marketing and insurance selling. Besides, reports also speak of ATMs are being used for topping up cash from one's account into smart card. Now ATMs are being used extensively for ticketing. For instance, it would be possible to book a movie ticket through an ATM. And the ticket would get printed and issued by the ATM itself. In the West, ticketing through ATM is more common than what it can be imagined in India.

Also any ATM user can request for the map of a particular area and get that printed for a charge from the very ATM itself.

Here is a survey result which shows the usage of ATM for different purposes.

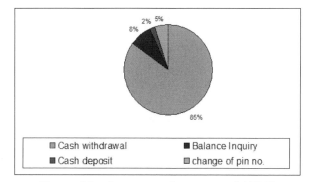

Figure 13 – Purpose-wise usage of ATMS

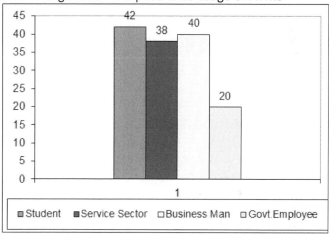

Figure 14 – ATM Usage by different section of Public

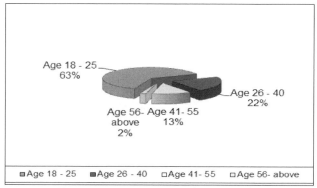

Figure 15 – ATM Usage by age-wise

6.5.2. ATM: Transaction Flow

Every time a customer walks into an ATM, inserts the card, punches a few keys and draws cash, a train of events happens. To understand what these are, let us take a real time example. Shabeer is a customer of XYZ Bank, holding a VISA Electron debit card issued by the bank. One fine day, he goes to PQR Bank's ATM which is near his residence and draws ₹10,000/- cash. Now let us see the transaction sequence as it gets triggered.

A. Shabeer inserts his card into the card reader and punches his PIN.
B. HDFC Bank's ATM forwards the PIN and other material details about the card issuer name, expiry date, etc., (embedded in the magnetic strip) to PQR Bank's switch.
C. PQR Bank's switch identifies the network/ issuer to which the card belongs and uses the "router table" information to send the input details to the acquiring bank (XYZ Bank) through the most optimal path.
D. On receipt of the input signal, the network forwards the same to the XYZ Bank (if XYZ Bank and PQR Bank are part of any shared payment network, the signal would travel to the hub of such an SPNS and would be routed to XYZ Bank).
E. XYZ Bank's processor verifies the PIN, authorizes the transaction, assigns a unique number to it and forwards the same to the network/ SPNS.
F. The network/ SPNS hub forwards the transaction authorisation details to PQR Bank's switch.
G. PQR Bank's switch, in turn, communicates to the ATM the authorisation details.
H. Shabeer keys in ₹10,000/- as the amount to be withdrawn.
I. ATM forwards the request to XYZ Bank's switch.
J. In turn, PQR Bank's switch forwards the request to the Network/ SPN.
K. Withdrawal request routed to XYZ Bank's processor (adding whatever fee that is payable by Shabeer for using a "foreign ATM" – here foreign does not mean overseas).
L. XYZ Bank acts upon the withdrawal request, forwards a debit authorisation to PQR Bank's switch through the network/ SPN.
M. The network forwards the withdrawal/ debit authorisation details to PQR Bank's switch.

N. PQR Bank's switch in turn forwards withdrawal authorisation to the ATM.

O. PQR Bank's ATM delivers the required currencies, spits out the card and prints a transaction receipt for delivery to Shabeer.

6.5.3. ATM Transactions: Settlement

While crisscross individual transactions are put through various ATMs of different banks by customers at various points of time, for a time bucket, settlement between banks in respect of all transactions would be on a consolidated/ batch basis at a designated time. To understand the settlement process, let us suppose a closed system that just has two banks. viz., XYZ Bank and PQR Bank and both have an arrangement by which their respective ATMs can be used by the customers of the other bank.

Given this, on any day, it is possible there would be a number of XYZ Bank customers who would have drawn cash from various ATMs of PQR Bank. Remember, this cash belongs to PQR Bank. Necessarily, therefore, XYZ Bank has to reimburse the same to PQR Bank. In addition, XYZ Bank would pay a "foreign ATM fee" to PQR Bank for letting its – XYZ Bank's – customers use ATMs owned by PQR Bank. Similarly, on the same day, it may happen that a number of customers of PQR Bank would have drawn cash from various ATMs of XYZ Bank. Here again, the cash belongs XYZ Bank and (along with the necessary "foreign ATM fee").

There would be a netting of these two opposite reimbursements and the net payable/ receivable 'amount would be communicated to the settlement agency (RBI), which would in turn debit/ credit the respective accounts of PQR Bank and XYZ Bank at the designated time.

Needless to say, the above is a very simplified version of reality. For, in any real time banking system, there are not just two banks. In fact, there are too many banks. And the crisscross transactional possibilities are phenomenal. Usually, in such a case, the netting would not stop at the bilateral stage between two banks. Instead, it could get extended to arrive at multilateral netting. And the multilateral net amount payable/ receivable would be debited/ credited to individual bank's accounts maintained with the settlement agency.

6.5.4. Exotic ATMs - A Globetrot

Even now, ATMs are under evolution. Techphobics would complain, 'over-evolution'. A series of exotic varieties are emerging day after day, each with one or more novel features. Think of a feature, it would have already found a place in one such ATM. The idea here is to catalogue some of the exotic ones.

There are ATMs, which are voice-guided. Also, there are ATMs which can voice-guide the customer. Such an ATM is very useful for visually challenged customers. In fact, in certain pockets of the US, there is a statutory stipulation that ATMs need to be voice-guiding so that their operation becomes easier for the visually impaired. But an ATM is not just a 'talk-and-listen' toy. Today, ATMs are also shrinking in size. Thus, one sees in the market Dwarf ATMs. Merchants with smaller room space are likely to go after them. And some ATMs in their obsession to get more and more dwarf are sacrificing their screens. But how does one transact with such 'ATMs sans screen'? Simple. The transaction requests can be shoot through the laptop/ digital phone/ personal digital assistant (PDA).

Of course, the most significant innovation comes from one of the vendors. It has designed and marketed an ATM that can recycle cash. Such an ATM can use the currencies deposited by one customer to meet the withdrawal request of another. Thus, from a bank's point of view, a recycling ATM could put through more transactions without seeking refill of its cash cassette. Likewise, from the perspective of a customer, cash deposits effected in a recycling ATM would be instantly counted, checked and credited to his/ her account. (In the case of other ATMs, cash deposits are effected using sealed covers and are not instantly credited to the account of the account holder]. Subject to cost factors recycling ATMs should have an overwhelming reception in the Southeast Asian countries as well as in India where, all said and done, still the economy is cash-driven. A word of caution though. As smart card culture picks up, recycling ATMs may lose some of their sheen and shine.

As the world is fast becoming a global village, it is inevitable that ATMs acquire the ability to handle more than one country's currency. In fact, they do now. A novel ATM that is being experimented by a company has the capacity to handle currencies of different denominations of say 25 countries. Needless to say, it would be able to exchange one country's currency for the other.

As things stand, ATMs function as standstill and static delivery channels. This is because, for communication purposes, most ATMs are using either dial-up or leased lines. Hence the first step required to make an ATM mobile is to arm it with wireless technology. In fact, wireless ATMs are already in use. One of the international ATM majors has come out with ATMs equipped with an infrared device that can establish a wireless like with a customer's wireless laptop, digital phone or PDA.

From wireless connectivity to mobility, it is a just short step away. No wonder, now there are ATMs which use all sorts of transport for their mobility. Hence, there are ATMs getting installed in long haul flights. Another unique feature of these ATMs is their ability to spit currencies of the flight's destination country. In the same way, ATMs have been deployed in cruise ships too. Of course, ATMs-on-wheels are an in-thing for quite some time now. In fact, ATMs-on-wheels could prove to be an effective substitute for a large cluster of branches. Besides, such ATMs-on-wheels are ideal for providing temporary banking services at a particular location during special events.

With their expanding functionality, ATMs are turning into kiosks. Besides functionality, color screen has also made ATM an amenable medium for advertising and targeted product promotion. In fact, ATMs are now being used for insurance selling and marketing mutual fund schemes.

One more development is, now there are web-enabled ATMs which can help users to put through net banking transactions too. In addition, some of the web-enabled and smart ATMs are capable of carrying out self-diagnosis and reporting problems through the net to the "control centre". Even as one concedes that PIN is the most widely used access control/

authentication mechanism, now there are ATMs which depend on biometrics for customer identification. For instance, a US-based credit union by name Riverside Health System Employees Credit Union has been making use of fingerprint scan for identification/ authentication of customers. Similarly, an American company has installed automated cashier machines that use "facial recognition" for access control/ identification. Of course, a lot of research is still on exploring the possibility of using Iris/ retina recognition for customer identification.

ATMs with touch screens have become quite common. Combining touch screen at the front end and expert systems at the backend, ATMs are being made 'intelligent'. Such ATMs are interactive and can offer investment advice to the users.

6.6. Chapter Summary

Convenience Users – Issuers' Curse! – Credit card industry has its own paradoxes. Here any card holder who promptly pays his/ her entire outstanding on receipt of periodic statements is not a welcome customer by the banks. They are unproductive for the banks. In fact card issuers refer to such card holders as "convenient users". For these cardholders generate very little revenue inasmuch as they offer literally no scope for charging interest in their credit card accounts. In fact, card issuers may even accuse that such cardholders get credit cards, but by their regular repayment behavior turn them into charge cards. All this without paying the usually higher service charges associated with charge cards. Hence next time around, if the credit card issuer gives a nasty stare even as the customer proudly effect full and prompt payment of the card outstanding, the customer don't be puzzled. For, in his/ her view the customer is a freeloader – the one who asks for a credit card, but ends up using it as a charge card.

➢ There are a host of cards that can be used for payment purposes.
➢ In the case of any credit card transaction, there are four parties to it: Issuer, acquirer, merchant and card holder. All card transactions are settled among banks using multilateral netting.

➤ ATMs represent the changing face of retail banking. In terms of functionality, ATMs prove versatile. As is the case with card transactions, ATM transactions too are settled among banks using multilateral netting.

*****

Chapter 7.   Other Banking Services

In general anyone will immediately list the general services of a bank as:

- Deposits
- Lending
- Payment System
- Remittance
- Card related activities, etc.

Besides the above, banks offer a host of services to their retail customers ranging from collection of cheques to rendering of investment advice. In fact, nowadays most banks focus as much on their "service window" as they do on the deposit and credit fronts. And there are banks which go the extra mile to satisfy their customers and sometimes tailor-make their services to suit a specific range of customers. When this happens to the extreme, retail banking metamorphoses into "Private Banking". In fact banks do involve themselves into various bouquets of other services like:

- Cheque Collection
- Remittance services
- Standing Orders/ Instructions
- Safe Deposit Lockers
- Safe Custody
- Private Banking
- Investment Research/ advice
- Portfolio Management Services
- Merchant Banking activities
- Demat account, etc.

7.1. Cheque Collection

In their capacity as agents of their customers, banks collect through the payment system the proceeds of cheques tendered by the customers and drawn on other banks. This is such a basic service that no bank can or does boast that it is offering this. Incidentally, a bank is not expected to offer this service to anyone who is not its customer. If it does, it could be only inviting some serious trouble. From an academic angle, collection of cheques by banks on behalf of their customers does not exactly fit within the classical functional definition of banking. Anyway it should be mentioned that if a bank were to confine itself to only the classical definition of banking, it would cease to exist in today's context.

7.2. Remittance Services

In the entire financial system, banks stand out because of one unique role they play — their ability to move money from one place to another and from one person to another. In fact, it is more or less impossible to think of moving money — except physical cash – without involving at least one bank and more often than not, at least two banks. Thus it is no wonder banks become the natural conduits for remittance of money for their customers. Some of the instruments being made available by banks to their customers for remittance purposes are: Demand Draft, Pay Order, Mail Transfer, Telegraphic Transfer, EFT, etc. In the case of remittance services, in most instances, banks offer such services to their customers as well as non–customers. In other words, there is no need for any banker-customer relationship for extension of this kind of service. Given the fact that this service proves to be a source of decent non-interest income for banks and that too without any risk, such a provision should definitely be music to their ears. In the Indian context, however, some banks may and do discriminate between their customers and non-customers when it comes to the amount of commission charge for such services. They may charge a higher amount of commission/ exchange from non-customers.

After the advent of core banking system, and new functionalities like any branch banking, EFT, RTGS, etc., some of the services like Mail Transfer, even collection of outstation cheques, etc., are not much used at present.

7.3. Standing Orders/ Instructions

For years, banks have been executing standing orders/ instructions given by their customers. Thus, a customer who would like his/ her bank to make rental payment every month can give a standing instruction to that effect. On the appointed date, the bank would debit his/ her account and remit the proceeds to the landlord. Of course, inasmuch as there is no free lunch in banking, banks charge some fee for extending such a service. More such instances are: periodical payment of interest on deposits, recent addition of Monthly Investment Plan of Mutual Funds, Payment of insurance premia, payment of locker rent, installments of Recurring Deposit and what not.

7.4. Safe Deposit Locker[7]

Most banks offer "safe deposit locker" facility to their customers. While no regulation prevents a bank from extending this service to non-customers too, anticipating certain practical problems, banks generally say no to such an arrangement. Thus, on regular payment of a certain amount of rent periodically, a customer can hire one or more of the locker cubicles/ boxes available within the bank's premises. Incidentally, when a customer avails himself/ herself of safe deposit locker facility, the relationship between him/ her and the bank is that of a tenant and a landlord. Needless to say, the bank offering the facility is the landlord, while the customer is the tenant.

7.4.1. Safe Deposit Lockers: How much safe are they for banks?

As is the case with most other retail services, banks generate healthy revenue by offering safe deposit facility to their customers. More than the absolute revenue, the collateral advantage which a bank/ branch derives by offering such a facility is immense. In fact, in competitive retail banking segment, this facility often used as a bait for attracting premium clients.

Nevertheless, there is a potential danger that awaits bank branches when they extend safe deposit locker facility to their customers. In the first place, there is no guarantee that all customers would use the lockers for legitimate purposes. Some of them may even safe-keep contraband items. But that is nothing compared to another serious risk posed to bank branches by safe deposit lockers. In a world populated by terrorists, there is a remote, but, at the same time a distinct possibility that dubious elements could misuse the safe deposit locker facility with devastating consequences. This is especially true when terrorism becomes endemic.

---

[7] In some countries, it is called Personal Safe Box Service

Given this, it appears that time has come; to revisit and amend the regulations relating to safe deposit lockers which can make them operationally safe for banks.

From a customer's point of view, the most attractive feature of the safe deposit locker facility is the fact he/ she can use the locker for safekeeping valuable items/ important documents. Besides, he/ she is not required to declare or exhibit to the bank what is being stored by him/ her in the locker. Banks, of course, may stipulate a negative restriction. Accordingly, for obvious reasons, explosives and such other dangerous materials cannot be stored in locker boxes! But, on the part of banks, it is difficult to verify the compliance of this condition by customers. The operational mechanism is so designed that no bank official can have access to any customer's locker box. In other words, customers can be assured of total secrecy *vis-à-vis* the contents stored in the locker boxes. Of course, given the operational mechanism, customers cannot hold the bank responsible for any loss/theft of articles kept/ purported to have been kept in safe deposit lockers. Banks would flatly refuse to take cognizance of such claims. Besides, given the fact that every locker cubicle has only one key which is given to the customer, if ever the key were to be lost, he/ she may have to pay through his/ her nose for getting the locker opened as well as for its eventual repair/ replacement. As in the case of deposit accounts, while availing themselves of safe deposit locker facility too, customers are entitled to nominate any person as the beneficiary. The person so nominated would be permitted to take possession of the contents of the safe deposit locker on the death of the customer. By the way, as is done in the case of deposit accounts, safe deposit lockers too can be operated singly or jointly. In any case, however, only one key would be handed over to the safe keepers.

Some private operators other than the commercial banks also do offer such services. In such cases the rent may be loaded with a little premium, but comes with 24 x 7 services. Customers need not depend on the timings of the banks for operating the lockers.

7.5. Safe Custody

Similar to safe deposit locker facility in objective but different in operational style, safe custody is a service being offered by most banks. Under this, a customer can handover any permissible article such as jewels, documents, etc., to the bank for safe custody on periodic payment of a fee. And the bank would keep the article/ document safe, would return the same to the customer on demand.

As could be observed, there is a material difference between safe deposit locker facility and — safe custody. In the latter case, the article is being handed over to the bank. In other words, the bank knows (and should know) what is being offered for safe custody. Besides, while in the case of safe deposit locker, the relationship between the banker and the customer is respectively that of a landlord and a tenant, in the matter of safe custody it is one of a bailer and a bailed. Yet another duty cast upon the bank under safe custody is that it has to return the article in the exact form in which the same has been originally received. In other words, if a customer were to offer an ancestral ornament weighing 200 Gms for safe custody, the bank cannot return 200 Gms of gold in biscuit form later when demanded by the customer and claim that it has done its duty. In other words, the duty of the bank is to safe keep the article "as is and how is".

Banks generally arrogate themselves the right to decide as to what kind of articles/ documents they would accept for safe custody. Else, they can find themselves in a nasty jam sometimes. Think of a customer offering a basket of rotten eggs, or still worse one box of RDX, for safe custody. As with safe deposit lockers, in the case of articles handed over for safe custody too, a customer can nominate any person of his/ her choice as the intended beneficiary in case of his/ her demise.

7.6. Private Banking

An understanding of retail banking would be incomplete without making least a passing reference about Private Banking and drawing a contrast between the two. As is well known, retail banking is about transacting with individual customers, catering to their various banking needs —

accepting deposits, lending and extending various other services. On the face of it, Private Banking is no different. For, it too deals with individual customers, providing an umbrella that takes care of their entire spectrum of banking, finance, investment and advisory requirements. But the similarity ends there.

Unlike retail banking, which in a sense is "mass banking", private banking is really "high class banking". Here the focus is on individuals with fairly huge to very huge net worth running into multi-millions of dollars in some cases. They are called High Net-worth Individuals in banking parlance. Thus, private bankers are more choosy and focused. Again, in private banking; individual transaction amounts are very large. Similarly, per account business turnover and profits are also very huge. Private banking also calls for the management of clients' estates, investing money on behalf of large value clients and managing their portfolios. In simple terms, it is a kind of "relationship banking" that demands extraordinary versatility and expertise on the part of private bankers. Given the kind of clients a bank deals with, the sensitivities involved are very fine in private banking. One slip here or a jerk there would mean not just the migration of the affected client account, but also the bank will have to face the reputational risk. This makes private banking business a tightrope walk, not meant for all and sundry banks.

In the International context, clients flock to private banks for two reasons. To let their finances be managed by professionals. That is one driver, but not the only one. Private banking offers a near total anonymity to the individual client. An attractive enough proposition for most high net worth individuals. Incidentally, some of the Swiss Banks primarily focus on "Private Banking". Thanks to some amenable Swiss laws and regulations, these banks have become postmasters in the art of veiling their clients.

7.7. Investment Research & Advice

For their retail customers, some of the banks set up dedicated windows for investment advice. In fact, this sort of service is mainly targeted at the nonresident clients and also for non-customers of the banks. The main intention is to expand customer base. For tendering such advice, banks also have equity/ market research wings manned by well-qualified specialists. However, there is a feeling that the banks do tend to market their products under the guise of Investment Advice. The customers should also use their knowledge to decide on the investments to save on.

7.8. Portfolio Management Services

Most well-established banks undertake to manage investments on behalf of their retail customers. This service is generally targeted at high net-worth individuals, especially nonresidents. Such portfolio management service can be offered in two styles:

> ➢ Discretionary Portfolio Management
> ➢ Non-Discretionary Portfolio Management.

As the name indicates, in the case of discretionary portfolio management, a corpus fund is given to the bank by the client. The bank has total operational discretion as to the individual shares/ securities which would be bought and sold on a day-to-day basis. The investor would only indicate his/ her overall investment objective and risk appetite. That is all.

On the other hand, in the case of non–discretionary portfolio management, the bank may advise a client as to the shares/ securities to be purchased/ sold. Nonetheless, the ultimate decision with respect to individual sale/ purchase would rest with the investor. Once the decision is conveyed by him/ her, the bank would just execute it.

Needless to say, non-discretionary portfolio management service is very restrictive from the bank's point of view. Besides, it would be utilised only by those clients who have a clearer understanding of the markets/ stocks. Conversely, discretionary portfolio management service is meant for those clients who have very little idea of the markets/ stocks/securities and thus would rather bank on the discretion and decision of their banks.

In the Indian context, banks were permitted to offer both discretionary and non-discretionary portfolio management services to their clients in the early 90s. However, owing to certain unhealthy practices resorted to by some banks, to the extent one understands, now discretionary portfolio management service offering by banks remains banned by RBI.

7.9. Merchant Banking Services

A **merchant bank** is a financial institution which provides capital to companies in the form of share ownership instead of loans. A merchant bank also provides advisory on corporate matters to the firms they lend to.

Today, according to the US Federal Deposit Insurance Corporation (FDIC), "the term merchant banking is generally understood to mean negotiated private equity investment by financial institutions in the unregistered securities of either privately or publicly held companies". Both commercial banks and investment banks may engage in merchant banking activities. Historically, merchant banks' original purpose was to facilitate and/or finance production and trade of commodities, hence the name 'merchant'. Few banks today restrict their activities to such a narrow scope. In some countries the Merchant Banking is also called as Investment Banking.

Merchant banks and investment banks, in their purest forms, are different kinds of financial institutions that perform different services. In practice, the fine lines that separate the functions of merchant banks and investment banks tend to blur. Traditional merchant banks often expand into the field of securities underwriting, while many investment banks participate in trade financing activities. In theory, investment banks and merchant banks perform different functions.

Pure investment banks raise funds for businesses and some governments by registering and issuing debt or equity and selling it on a market. Traditionally, investment banks only participated in underwriting and selling securities in large blocks. Investment banks facilitate mergers and acquisitions through share sales and provide research and financial consulting to companies. Traditionally, investment banks did not deal with the general public.

Traditional merchant banks primarily perform international financing activities such as foreign corporate investing, foreign real estate investment, trade finance and international transaction facilitation. Some of the activities that a pure merchant bank is involved in may include issuing letters of credit, transferring funds internationally, trade consulting and co-investment in projects involving trade of one form or another.

The current offerings of investment banks and merchant banks varies by the institution offering the services, but there are a few characteristics that most companies that offer both investment and merchant banking share.

As a general rule, investment banks focus on initial public offerings (IPOs) and large public and private share offerings. Merchant banks tend to operate on small-scale companies and offer creative equity financing, bridge financing, mezzanine financing and a number of corporate credit products. While investment banks tend to focus on larger companies, merchant banks offer their services to companies that are too big for venture capital firms to serve properly, but are still too small to make a compelling public share offering on a large exchange. In order to bridge the gap between venture capital and a public offering, larger merchant banks tend to privately place equity with other financial institutions, often taking on large portions of ownership in companies that are believed to have strong growth potential.

Merchant banks still offer trade financing products to their clients. Investment banks rarely offer trade financing because most investment banking clients have already outgrown the need for trade financing and the various credit products linked to it.

The only service Merchant Banks/ Investment banks do offer to retail customers is that they accept application for IPOs and also provide the service of ABSA (Application Supported by Blocked Amount) – in the sense the customers need not pay the money to the corporates alongwith the share application itself. The money is separately kept with the merchant/ investment banks and earmarked for the IPO. Once the IPO is allotted the money is paid to the corporate and interest is paid to the customers. If the IPO is not allotted to the customer then the entire money with interest is returned to the customer.

7.10. Demat Account

About 1.5 decades back in India, till around mid 90s, shares and other securities used to be issued in paper form and for every purchase and sale in the market, the ownership will be transferred in that paper.

The term 'demat', refers to a dematerialised form of securities like listed stocks or debentures in electronic form rather than paper, as required for investors. In a demat account, shares and securities are held electronically instead of the investor taking physical possession of certificates. A demat account is opened by the investor while registering with an investment broker (or sub-broker). The demat account number is quoted for all transactions to enable electronic settlements of trades to take place.

Instead of investment brokers most of the commercial banks also have started to offer Demat account services to the retail customers. In a crude way if we compare the savings accounts and demat accounts – the money is credited or debited while depositing or withdrawing from savings accounts. Similarly shares are credited or debited in a demat account while purchasing or selling of the concerned share. This makes the operation easier and e-based operation is also possible.

There are lot of benefits of demat. Some of them are:

- Easy and convenient way to hold securities
- Immediate transfer of securities
- No stamp duty on transfer of securities
- Safer than paper-shares (earlier risks associated with physical certificates such as bad delivery, fake securities, delays, thefts etc. are mostly eliminated)

- Reduced paperwork for transfer of securities
- Reduced transaction cost
- No "odd lot" problem: even one share can be sold
- Change in address recorded with a depository participant gets registered with all companies in which investor holds securities eliminating the need to correspond with each of them separately.
- Transmission of securities is done by depository participant, eliminating the need for notifying companies.
- Automatic credit into demat account for shares arising out of bonus/ split, consolidation/ merger, etc.
- A single demat account can hold investments of all equity, debt, etc., instruments. Nowadays gold and other commodities also have been started to be Demat form.
- Traders can work from anywhere across the globe.

7.11.   Chapter Summary

In addition to deposit accounts and credit facilities, banks offer a basket of services to their retail customers. These are:

- ➢ Cheque collection
- ➢ Remittance service
- ➢ Card issue
- ➢ Standing orders
- ➢ Safe deposit lockers
- ➢ Safe custody facility
- ➢ Investment research & advice
- ➢ Portfolio management services.

*****

Chapter 8.   Financial Inclusion

Financial inclusion is the concept, which is couple of decades old. Even it can very well be called as 21st Century banking. Its main is aim to take banking system to remote areas where banking is not even heard of. Financial inclusion or inclusive financing is the delivery of financial services at affordable costs to sections of disadvantaged and low income segments of society. Unrestrained access to public goods and services is the sine qua non of an open and efficient society. It is argued that as banking services are in the nature of public good, it is essential that availability of banking and payment services to the entire population without discrimination is the prime objective of public policy. The term "financial inclusion" has gained importance since the early 00s, and is a result of findings about financial exclusion and its direct correlation to poverty. Financial inclusion is now a common objective for central banks of many developing nations.

8.1.   Introduction

Financial Inclusion (FI) is enabling access to/ delivery of banking services at an affordable cost to the vast sections of disadvantaged and low-income groups. Unrestrained access to public goods and services is the sine qua non of public policy of a nation. As banking services are in the nature of public service, provision of banking and payment services to the entire population without discrimination should be the prime objective of the public policy.

The spread of banking facilities, though impressive, has been uneven in the country, throwing up challenges for achieving financial inclusion. In fact, despite impressive growth of branch network in India, the vast sections of the society remain financially excluded and continue to remain away from the formal system and thereby access to financial services including savings, credit and insurance. The banking industry in India has shown tremendous growth in volume and complexity during the last couple of decades. The country has an extensive banking infrastructure comprising around 35,000 rural and semi-urban branches of commercial banks, over 15,000 branches of Regional Rural Banks, around 12,000 branches of District Central Co-operative Banks and nearly 1,00,000 cooperatives credit societies at the village level. There is at least one retail credit outlet on an average for about 5,000 rural people, which translates into one outlet for every 1,000 households. This is a remarkable and extensive work. Given this network the moot question would be "Are the financial service needs of the rural poor comprehensively met by this network?"

The picture is none too impressive, going by the available data on the number of savings accounts and even assuming that one person has only one account, on an all India basis only 59 per cent of adult population in the country has bank accounts. The un-banked population is higher in the North Eastern and Eastern Regions as compared to other regions.

Further, the extent of credit inclusion is even lower at 14 per cent of adult population. The financially excluded sections largely comprise marginal farmers, landless labourers, oral lessees, self-employed and unorganised sector enterprises, urban slum dwellers, migrants, ethnic minorities and socially excluded groups, senior citizens and women. The statistics were compiled taking India into consideration. But this is all the more true in most of the countries excepting so called developed countries, where the picture may be a little different.

8.2.   Background

Bangladesh has been acknowledged as a pioneer in the field of micro-finance. Dr. Muhammad Yunus[8], Professor of Economics in Chittagong University of Bangladesh, was an initiator of an action research project 'Grameen Bank'. The project started in later 70s and it was formally recognised as a bank through an ordinance, issued by the government in early 80s. Even then it does not have a scheduled status from the Central bank of the country, the Bangladesh Bank. The Grameen Bank provides loans to the landless poor, particularly women, to promote self-employment. At the start of 00s, it had a membership of 23.78 lakh and cumulative micro-credit disbursements of Tk 14.653 Crores.

---

[8] He was awarded Nobel Peace Prize in the year 2006

8.3.   Microfinance and Financial Inclusion

Microfinance programmes are intended to reach poor segments of society as they lack access to financial services. It, therefore, holds greater promise to further the agenda of financial inclusion as it seeks to reach out to the excluded category of population from the banking system. The predominant micro finance programme namely SHG bank linkage programme has demonstrated across the country its effectiveness in linking banks with excluded category of poor segments of population. In this process, the role of development NGOs is quite pronounced in providing the last mile connectivity as enablers and catalyst between the SHGs/ Village level co-operatives and the banks. This is also supplemented by the MFIs delivering credit.

The importance of financial literacy and financial counseling as essential component of the financial inclusion also needs to be recognised. In pursuit of the financial inclusion, there are many issues and challenges both on the access and affordability – the two pillars of the financial inclusion, besides expanding reach to the triad of basic financial services like savings, credit and insurance – payment system and the sustainability of the inclusion process are also essential.

8.4.   Connecting People with Banking System

This is aimed through SHG Bank Linkage Programme. Given the experience so far in promoting financial inclusion through SHG bank linkage there is a need to appreciate and recognize the following financial inclusion is not just credit dispensation, its about connecting the people with the banking system for availing bouquet of financial services including access to payment system. The critical issue, in the first place, is to connect and the SHG bank linkage programme since the 90s rank is, by far, the major programme initiative without parallel in any parts of the world for the financial inclusion. The uniqueness of the SHG Bank Linkage programme lies in the fact that it is not mere delivery of financial services but is an inherent design for promoting financial literacy. As the financial literacy increases, the financial inclusion gets more sustainability and stability in terms of being inclusive on a long haul.

SHG bank linkage by far is an effective instrument for financial inclusion. Considering the importance of linkage the bank accounts of SHGs provide the first link for the members of SHG for graduation and then to individual family accounts in due course. This process need to be respected and encouraged to facilitate informed inclusion process. That opening of bank accounts (Savings) is the beginning of beginning of the financial inclusion process, which is a mean to achieve larger end of financial inclusion.

To achieve faster spread of financial inclusion, it is vital that the stake holders and it particular commercial bank recognize the need to take the banking services with the technological support to the people rather than waiting for the people to reach out to the banks.

8.5.   Technological initiatives for FI

Technology holds the key to further the process of financial inclusion, more so in the remote and far flung areas. It enhances access to financial services in a cost effective manner and over time with the increasing volume lead to more affordability. The challenge lies in making the technologies friendlier to the illiterate clients from the poor segments of the society, who are normally excluded from the financial system. Some of the initiatives which are currently under way on experimental basis are worth mentioning:

- ATMs with operating instructions in vernacular language facilitating the access for the poor people with reading disability
- ATMs with voice recognition for the illiterates for transactions relating to savings, credit and payment services
- Bio metric enabled ATMs to bring more illiterate poor to the banking fold
- Mobile teller/ low cost ATMs in the remote areas
- KIOSK banking using the internet facility

8.6. Indian Scenario

India has adopted the Bangladesh's model in a modified form. To alleviate the poverty and to empower the women, the micro-finance has emerged as a powerful instrument in the new economy. With availability of micro-finance, self-help groups (SHGs) and credit management groups have also started in India. And thus the movement of SHG has spread out in India. More importance is being given to SHGs, since the micro lending to the group rather than individual borrowers is more successful. All the members of the group are equally benefitted and also the repayment by each member is guaranteed by all other members of the group. Hence the repayment is almost 100%. The members are also benefitted from clutches of individual lenders who were charging predominantly high rate of interest and also take every possible initiative for recovery. All the more the entire initiative of micro lending depends on Women SHGs, which was found to be grand success in Bangladesh.

8.7. Business Process

Below mentioned is a generic business process which may slightly vary from country to country and even within the same country, between bank to bank.

Under this scheme, Banks are outsourcing the entire operations, though it still owns the end customer accounts. The accounts under the scheme are not normal accounts and cannot be operated through normal bank branches or any of the ATMS and other infrastructure. The total amount of transactions (deposits) for an account should not exceed a threshold limit say ₹50,000/- per annum. In case it exceeds the amount, the operations have to be shifted to branches.

Under this scheme Banks identify a Business Consultant (BC) and outsource these operations. The Business consultants in turn will have Customer Service Points (CSP) who can be self-help groups at village levels or any voluntary organisations. These CSPs are the ones who will be actually in touch with the rural people and distribute the pensions, wages or collect deposits etc. These will be trained by BCs. Banks have an agreement with a technical partner as BC to provide technical solution for banking facilities to rural community through Women Self Help Group Members and Technical Partner works with self-help groups at village level to do actual transactions. Technical Partner works with Bank on revenue sharing basis. Here one of the Technical Partners collaborated with Nxp semiconductors to design a mobile application for the Government that encloses an RFID card that works with Technical Partner's micro banking platform Zero Mass Environment. Some of the devices used are:

- Biometric enabled Smart Card, currently stores customer Account Number and the 6 finger scans of the customer.
- New Field Communication (NFC) enabled Mobile set with proprietary application to perform transaction and capture customer registration data.
- Finger Print scanner, to capture and authenticate the customer.
- Printer, to print the transaction receipts.
- Camera, to capture the customer photograph and an image of the customer application form.
- Data collection device, to consolidate the captured customer data during registration process and transfer it to the central card personalisation unit.
- Data server-Service Provider, to receive and transmit the customer transaction thrice a day from the mobile handsets of CSP's and once to Bank server.
- Data server-Bank, to receive/ transmit transaction from service provider server.

Figure 16 – Devices used in a typical FI

8.8. Operation Process Involved

Like business process mentioned above, this operational process described below is a generic one. Zero MASS acts as Business Consultant (BC) who will perform the following activities in the villages:

- Appoints Customer Service Providers (CSP) to perform tiny card services to the community.
- All CSPs must be members of any Self Help Group of that village. Only women are considered as CSPs. They must be permanent residents of that village. To ensure this, only daughter-in-laws of the village are considered.
- Zero Mass conducts and selects the CSPs based on a written exam. All the selected candidates will be trained to operate the mobile, finger print scanner, Thermo printer and Digital camera.
- Zero Mass will provide technical support people to resolve any technical issues pertaining to the mobile instruments like battery failures, software problems, wrong key pressing, etc.
- CSPs will perform the following preparation of applications for Smart card account:
  - o The application is pre-filled with the data received from NREGS and PPOs.
  - o The customer service provider (CSP) will obtain the following details of the customer:

- o Take photo of the account holder along with the barcode available on the application form using a digital camera
- o Take finger prints of Thumb, Index and middle fingers of both hands using a finger print scanner.
- o Application is filled in consultation with customer
- o The application is scanned and sent to Technical Partner for personalisation. The original application is sent to the nearest Bank branch to open the account.

- A Technical Partner sends the data received from BC to the dedicated accounts unit (DAU) of Bank.
- DAU of Bank sends the data to the relevant nearby branch. The branch will validate the data by comparing with the original application already available with them.
- Upon validation, the branch sends the confirmation back to DAU who in turn sends the same to Central Data Server (CDS) of Bank to open the accounts.
- Each tiny card will be given a 16 digit account number. This information is sent to Technical Partner for further processing of card. In future, the account numbers will be modified to 11 digits as a part of core banking solution. The branches, therefore, have reduced transaction loads, and no settlement or collection risk is carried by the bank.
- Full traceability and audit trail of the transaction is maintained.
- All CSPs will also carry a Smart card for authorisation to perform the banking   operations in mobile. The cards will have the following features:
  - o Passive RFID tag containing the name of the CSP, finger print information, etc.
  - o Photo of the CSP printed on the front side of the card.
  - o CSP id number printed on the front side of the card.
- Zero mass will supplement the cash requirements to CSPs every Saturday.

8.9.   Issues and Challenges

Typical of any new initiatives there are lot of Issues and Challenges in the case Financial Inclusion also.

- The vast segments of population particularly poor segment of society are out of the formal financial system. The financial inclusion process should take the banking services to the poor rather than poor people coming to the bank for availing the services.
- For sustaining the financial inclusion, the financial literacy becomes a very critical component. There is a need to simultaneously focus on the financial literacy part besides the delivery/ access.
- Penetration of insurance services – Insurance services largely remain as the urban phenomena. It should reach out to the rural and remote areas and to the poor segments of the societies. Micro Insurance Services should be given greater importance while extending the financial services.
- Cost effective technologies and applications in appropriate manner.
- Access to payment services through technology.
- Regional imbalances in the financial inclusion process is quite visible and there is a need for the microfinance movement to reach broader India, for that matter any country, to make the financial inclusion more meaningful and inclusive.
- Cash management and handling is one of the problems faced by Bank. When the operations grows, meeting the demand of physical cash requirements and depositing excess cash in banks is seen to be an operational issue that need to be addressed.
- Presently the user authentication is to be done through finger printing and matching which will be 90% reliable. This authentication process need to be improved to make it foolproof and system should be able to identify the right person who is illiterate.
- Because of lack of communications, uploading/ downloading of the data is a challenge. Currently the CSP is going to nearby hill or top of the building or any highest place to upload or download the data to servers. This is one issue that needs to be improved.
- Identification of the cardholder for re-issue of card in case he/ she loses/ damage the card given to him/ her; keeping in view they are illiterate and they cannot provide the number.
- One can never be sure how the requirements will scale up to meet the growth in transactions and whether the technology can meet up the requirements.

- Currently the upload/ download of the data takes place over GPRS to servers. This solution may not be a secure one. When the solution is blown up, data security needs to be beefed up.

8.10.   Chapter Summary

➢ FI is basically delivery of financial services at an affordable cost to vast sections of disadvantaged and low income groups.
➢ Financial Services include:
   o Savings
   o Credit
   o Insurance
   o Remittance Facilities, etc.
➢ Advantages to FI
   o Reduction in transactions costs of savers
   o Reduction in transactions costs of banks
   o Low risk cost
   o Appropriate products
➢ Who are covered by FI?
   o Marginal/ Landless Farmers
   o Self Employed
   o Urban slum developers
   o Minorities/ Migrants
   o Social excluded groups
   o Senior citizens
   o Women

*****

Chapter 9.   Islamic Banking

Islamic banking is relatively a new concept – say less than half a century old and is still evolving. Obviously this would be practiced by banks in Islamic countries. There are more grey areas especially when the banks in Islamic countries want to transact with banks in non-Islamic countries. However, let us discuss some concepts being followed in this area.

9.1.   Introduction

Modern banking system was introduced into the Muslim countries at a time when they were politically and economically at low ebb, in the late 19th Century. The main banks in the home countries of the imperial powers established local branches in the capitals of the subject countries and they catered mainly to the import export requirements of the foreign businesses. The banks were generally confined to the capital cities and the local population remained largely untouched by the banking system. The local trading community avoided the 'foreign' banks both for nationalistic as well as religious reasons. However, as time went on, it became difficult to engage in trade and other activities without making use of commercial banks. Even then many confined their involvement to transaction activities such as current accounts and money transfers. Borrowing from the banks and depositing their savings with the bank were strictly avoided in order to keep away from dealing in interest which is prohibited by religion.

With the passage of time, however, and other socio-economic forces demanding more involvement in national economic and financial activities, avoiding the interaction with the banks became impossible. Local banks were established on the same lines as the interest-based foreign banks for want of another system and they began to expand within the country bringing the banking system to more local people. As countries became independent the need to engage in banking activities became unavoidable and urgent. Governments, businesses and individuals began to transact business with the banks, with or without liking it. This state of affairs drew the attention and concern of Muslim intellectuals. The story of interest-free or Islamic banking begins here. In the following paragraphs this story has been traced to date and examined as to how far and how successfully the concerns have been addressed. For the benefit of the readers, a list of commonly used Islamic Banking terms is provided in Appendix 1.

9.2. Historical development

It seems that the history of interest-free banking could be divided into two parts. First, when it still remained an idea; second, when it became a reality — by private initiative in some countries and by law in others. The two periods are discussed separately. The last decade has seen a marked decline in the establishment of new Islamic banks and the established banks seem to have failed to live up to the expectations. The literature of the period begins with evaluations and ends with attempts at finding ways and means of correcting and overcoming the problems encountered by the existing banks.

9.2.1. Interest-free banking as an idea

In two decades (1950s and 60s) interest-free banking attracted more attention, partly because of the political interest it created in Pakistan and partly because of the emergence of young Muslim economists. Works specifically devoted to this subject began to appear in this period.
Early seventies saw the institutional involvement. Conference of the Finance Ministers of the Islamic Countries held in Karachi in 1970, the Egyptian study in 1972, First International Conference on Islamic Economics in Mecca in 1976, International Economic Conference in London in 1977 were the result of such involvement. The involvement of institutions and governments led to the application of theory to practice and resulted in the establishment of the first interest-free banks. The Islamic Development Bank, an inter-governmental bank established in 1975, was born of this process.

9.2.2. Interest-free banks in practice

The first private interest-free bank, the Dubai Islamic Bank, was also set up in 1975 by a group of Muslim businessmen from several countries. Two more private banks were founded in 1977 under the name of Faisal Islamic Bank in Egypt and the Sudan. In the same year the Kuwaiti government set up the Kuwait Finance House.

In the ten years since the establishment of the first private commercial bank in Dubai, more than 50 interest-free banks have come into being. Though nearly all of them are in Muslim countries, there are some in Western Europe as well: in Denmark, Luxembourg, Switzerland and the UK. Many banks were established in 1983 (11) and 1984 (13). The numbers have declined considerably in the following years.

In most countries the establishment of interest-free banking had been by private initiative and were confined to that bank. In Iran and Pakistan, however, it was by government initiative and covered all banks in the country. The governments in both these countries took steps in 1981 to introduce interest-free banking. In Pakistan, effective 1 January 1981 all domestic commercial banks were permitted to accept deposits on the basis of profit-and-loss sharing (PLS). New steps were introduced on 1 January 1985 to formally transform the banking system over the next six months to one based on no interest. From 1 July 1985 no banks could accept any interest bearing deposits, and all existing deposits became subject to PLS rules. Yet some operations were still allowed to continue on the old basis. In Iran, certain administrative steps were taken in February 1981 to eliminate interest from banking operations. Interest on all assets was replaced by a 4 percent maximum service charge and by a 4 to 8 percent 'profit' rate depending on the type of economic activity. Interest on deposits was also converted into a 'guaranteed minimum profit.' In August 1983 the Usury-free Banking Law was introduced and a fourteen-month change over period began in January 1984. The whole system was converted to an interest-free one in March 1985.

9.3.   Current practices

Generally speaking, all interest-free banks agree on the basic principles. However, individual banks differ in their applications. These differences are due to several reasons including the laws of the country, objectives of the different banks, individual bank's circumstances and experiences, the need to interact with other interest-based banks, etc. The salient features common to all banks are discussed below.

9.3.1. Deposit accounts

All the Islamic banks have three kinds of deposit accounts: current, savings and investment.

9.3.2. Current accounts

Current or demand deposit accounts are virtually the same as in all conventional banks. Deposit is guaranteed.

9.3.3. Savings accounts

Savings deposit accounts operate in different ways. In some banks, the depositors allow the banks to use their money but they obtain a guarantee of getting the full amount back from the bank. Banks adopt several methods of inducing their clients to deposit with them, but no profit is promised. In others, savings accounts are treated as investment accounts but with less stringent conditions as to withdrawals and minimum balance. Capital is not guaranteed but the banks take care to invest money from such accounts in relatively risk-free short-term projects. As such lower profit rates are expected and that too only on a portion of the average minimum balance on the ground that a high level of reserves needs to be kept at all times to meet withdrawal demands.

9.3.4. Investment account

Investment deposits are accepted for a fixed or unlimited period of time and the investors agree in advance to share the profit (or loss) in a given proportion with the bank. Capital is not guaranteed.

9.4.   Modes of financing

Banks adopt several modes of acquiring assets or financing projects. But they can be broadly categorised into three areas: investment, trade and lending.

9.4.1. Investment financing

This is done in three main ways:

- *Musharaka* where a bank may join another entity to set up a joint venture, both parties participating in the various aspects of the project in varying degrees. Profit and loss are shared in a pre-arranged manner. This is not very different from the joint venture concept. The venture is an independent legal entity and the bank may withdraw gradually after an initial period.
- *Mudarabha* where the bank contributes the finance and the client provides the expertise, management and labour. Profits are shared by both the partners in a pre-arranged proportion, but when a loss occurs the total loss is borne by the bank.
- Financing on the basis of an *estimated rate of return*. Under this scheme, the bank estimates the expected rate of return on the specific project it is financing and provides financing on the understanding that at least that rate is payable to the bank. (Perhaps this rate is negotiable.) If the project ends up in a profit more than the estimated rate the excess goes to the client. If the profit is less than the estimate the bank will accept the lower rate. In case a loss is suffered the bank will take a share in it.

9.4.2. Trade financing

This is also done in several ways. The main ones are:

- *Mark-up* where the bank buys an item for a client and the client agrees to repay the bank the price and an agreed profit later on.
- *Leasing* where the bank buys an item for a client and leases it to him for an agreed period and at the end of that period the lessee pays the balance on the price agreed at the beginning and becomes the owner of the item.
- *Hire-purchase* where the bank buys an item for the client and hires it to him for an agreed rent and period, and at the end of that period the client automatically becomes the owner of the item.

- *Sell-and-buy-back* where a client sells one of his properties to the bank for an agreed price payable now on condition that he will buy the property back after certain time for an agreed price.
- *Letters of credit* where the bank guarantees the import of an item using its own funds for a client, on the basis of sharing the profit from the sale of this item or on a mark-up basis.

9.4.3. Lending

Main forms of Lending are:

- *Loans with a service charge* where the bank lends money without interest but they cover their expenses by levying a service charge. This charge may be subject to a maximum set by the authorities.
- *No-cost loans* where each bank is expected to set aside a part of their funds to grant no-cost loans to needy persons such as small farmers, entrepreneurs, producers, etc. and to needy consumers.
- *Overdrafts* also are to be provided, subject to a certain maximum, free of charge.

9.5.   Services

Other banking services such as money transfers, bill collections, trade in foreign currencies at spot rate etc. where the bank's own money is not involved are provided on a commission or charges basis.

9.6.   Shortcomings in current practices

The current practices under three categories listed above: deposits, modes of financing (or acquiring assets) and services. There seems to be no problems as far as banking services are concerned. Islamic banks are able to provide nearly all the services that are available in the conventional banks. The only exception seems to be in the case of letters of credit where there is a possibility for interest involvement. However some solutions have been found for this problem – mainly by having excess liquidity with the foreign bank. On the deposit side, judging by the volume of deposits both in the countries where both systems are available and in countries where law prohibits any dealing in interest, the non-payment of interest on deposit accounts seems to be no serious problem. Customers still seem to deposit their money with interest-free banks.

The main problem, both for the banks and for the customers, seems to be in the area of financing. Bank lending is still practised but that is limited to either no-cost loans (mainly consumer loans) including overdrafts, or loans with service charges only. Both these types of loans bring no income to the banks and therefore naturally they are not that keen to engage in this activity much. That leaves us with investment financing and trade financing. Islamic banks are expected to engage in these activities only on a profit and loss sharing (PLS) basis. This is where the banks' main income is to come from and this is also from where the investment account holders are expected to derive their profits from. And the latter is supposed to be the incentive for people to deposit their money with the Islamic banks. And it is precisely in this PLS scheme that the main problems of the Islamic banks lay. Therefore this system has to be more carefully looked into in the following sections.

9.7.   The PLS scheme

An overview of the profit and loss sharing scheme of Islamic Banking in three different areas are highlighted below. This shows how Islamic banking is different from conventional banking – where interest is paid or charged.

9.7.1.   Savings accounts and capital guarantee

As the name itself indicates the primary aim of the saving account depositor is the safe-keeping of the savings. It is correctly perceived by the conventional banker and he guarantees the return of the deposit *intoto*. The banker also assumes that the depositor will prefer to keep his money with him in preference to another who might also provide the same guarantee, if the depositor is provided an incentive. This incentive is called interest and this interest is made proportional to the amount and length of time it is left with the bank in order to encourage more money brought into the bank and left there for longer periods of time. In addition, the interest rate is fixed in advance so that the depositor and the banker are fully aware of their respective rights and obligations from the beginning. And laws have been enacted to guarantee their enforcement. In Economic theory the interest is often taken to be the 'compensation' the depositors demand and receive for parting with their savings. The fact that the depositors accept the paid interest and that, given other things being equal, they prefer the bank or the scheme which offers the highest interest proves the banker's assumption correct.

The situation is very different in the Islamic banks. Here too the depositor's first aim is to keep his savings in safe custody. Islamic bankers divide the conventional savings account into two categories (alternatively, create a new kind of account):

- Savings Account
- Investment Account

The investment accounts operate fully under the PLS scheme – capital is not guaranteed, neither is there any pre-fixed return. Under the savings account the nominal value of the deposit is guaranteed, but they receive no further guaranteed returns. Banks may consider funds under the savings accounts too as part of their resources and use it to create assets. This is theory. In practice, however, the banks prefer, encourage and emphasise the investment accounts. This is because since their assets operate under the PLS scheme they might incur losses on these assets which they cannot pass onto the savings accounts depositors on account of the capital guarantee on these accounts. In the process the first aim of the depositor is pushed aside and the basic rule of commercial banking – capital guarantee – is broken.

It is suggested that all Islamic banks guarantee the capital under their savings accounts. This will satisfy the primary need and expectation of an important section of the depositors and, in Muslim countries where both Islamic and conventional banks co-exist, will induce more depositors to bank with the Islamic banks. At the same time, it will remove the major objection to establishing Islamic banks in non-Muslim countries.

9.7.2. Loans with a service charge

The problems of the Islamic banks arise from their need to acquire their assets under the PLS scheme. A simple solution does, in fact, already exist in the current theories of Islamic banking. It need only be pointed out and acted upon. There are three different viz. Iranian, Pakistani and the Siddiqi models in this regard.

All three models provide for loans with a service charge. Though the specific rules are not identical, the principle is the same. It is suggested that the funds in the deposit accounts (current and savings) be used to grant loans (short- and long-term) with a service charge. By doing this the Islamic banks will be able to provide all the loan facilities that conventional banks provide while giving capital guarantee for depositors and earning an income for themselves. Furthermore, and it is important, they can avoid all the problems. This would also remove the rest of the obstacles in opening and operating Islamic banks in non-Muslim countries.

The bonus for the borrowers is that the service charge levied by the Islamic banks will necessarily be less than the interest charged by conventional banks.

The existing relevant rules in the three models:

Model 1 – The Iranian model provides for *Gharz-al hasaneh* whose definition, purpose and operation are given in Articles 15, 16 and 17 of Regulations relating to the granting of banking facilities:

Article 15 – Gharz-al-hasaneh is a contract in which one (the lender) of the two parties relinquishes a specific portion of his possessions to the other party (the borrower) which the borrower is obliged to return to the lender in kind or, where not possible, its cash value.

Article 16 – The banks shall set aside a part of their resources and provide Gharz-al-hasaneh for the following purposes:

- To provide equipment, tools and other necessary resources so as to enable the creation of employment, in the form of co-operative bodies, for those who lack the necessary means;
- To enable expansion in production, with particular emphasis on agricultural, livestock and industrial products;
- To meet essential needs.

Article 17 – The expenses incurred in the provision of Gharz-al-hasaneh shall be, in each case, calculated on the basis of the directives issued by the Central bank and collected from the borrower.

Model 2 – In Pakistan, permissible modes of financing include:

Financing by lending:
- Loans not carrying any interest on which the banks may recover a service charge not exceeding the proportionate cost of the operation, excluding the cost of funds and provisions for bad and doubtful debts. The maximum service charge permissible to each bank will be determined by the State Bank from time to time.
- Qard-e-hasana loans given on compassionate grounds free of any interest or service charge and repayable if and when the borrower is able to pay.

Model 3 – Siddiqi has suggested that 50 percent of the funds in the 'deposit' (i.e. current and savings) accounts be used to grant short-term loans. A fee is to be charged for providing these loans:

An appropriate way of levying such a fee would be to require prospective borrowers to pay a fixed amount on each application, regardless of the amount required, the term of the loan or whether the application is granted or rejected. Then the applicants to whom a loan is granted may be required to pay an additional prescribed fee for all the entries made in the banks registers. The criterion for fixing the fees must be the actual expenditure which the banks have incurred in scrutinising the applications and making decisions, and in maintaining accounts until loans are repaid. These fees should not be made a source of income for the banks, but regarded solely as a means of maintaining and managing the interest-free loans.

It is clear from the above that all three models agree on the need for having cash loans as one mode of financing, and that this service should be paid for by the borrower. Though the details may vary, all seem to suggest that the charge should be the absolute cost only. It can be suggested that a percentage of this absolute cost be added to the charge as a payment to the bank for providing this service. This should enable an Islamic bank to exist and function independently of its performance in its PLS operations.

9.7.3.   Investment under PLS scheme

The idea of participatory financing introduced by the Islamic banking movement is a unique and positive contribution to modern banking. However, as seen earlier, by making the PLS mode of financing the main (often almost the only) mode of financing the Islamic banks have run into several difficulties. If, as suggested in the previous section, the Islamic banks would provide all the conventional financing through lending from their deposit accounts (current and savings), it will leave their hands free to engage in this responsible form of financing innovatively, using the funds in their investment accounts. They could then engage in genuine *Mudaraba* financing. Being partners in an enterprise they will have access to its accounts, and the problems associated with the non-availability of accounts will not arise.

9.8.   Problems in implementing the PLS scheme

Several schools of thought were put forth, with varying degrees of success, that Islamic Banking based on the concept of profit and loss sharing (PLS) is theoretically superior to conventional banking from different angles. However from the practical point of view things do not seem that rosy concerning everyone. In the over half-a-decade of full-scale experience in implementing the PLS scheme the problems have begun to show up. Some of the major difficulties in different areas are:

9.8.1.   Financing

There are four main areas where the Islamic banks find it difficult to finance under the PLS scheme:

- Participating in long-term low-yield projects
- Financing the small businessman
- Granting non-participating loans to running businesses
- Financing government borrowing

9.8.1.1.   Long-term projects

Less than 10 percent of the total assets go into medium and long-term investment. Admittedly, the banks were unable or unwilling to participate in long-term projects. The main reason is the need to participate in the enterprise on a PLS basis, which involves time consuming complicated assessment procedures and negotiations, requiring expertise and experience. There are no commonly accepted criteria for project evaluation based on PLS partnerships. Each single case has to be treated separately with utmost care and each has to be assessed and negotiated on its own merits. Other obvious reasons are:

- Such investments tie up capital for very long periods, unlike in conventional banking where the capital is recovered in regular instalments almost right from the beginning, and the uncertainty and risk are that much higher
- The longer the maturity of the project, the longer it takes to realise the returns and the banks therefore cannot pay a return to their depositors as quick as the conventional banks can.

Thus it is no wonder that the banks gave lesser priority to such investments.

9.8.1.2.   Small businesses

Small scale businesses form a major part of a country's productive sector. Besides, they form a greater number of the banks' clientele. Yet it seems difficult to provide them with the necessary financing under the PLS scheme, even though there is excess liquidity in the banks.

Given the comprehensive criteria to be followed in granting loans and monitoring their use by banks, small-scale enterprises have, in general encountered greater difficulties in obtaining financing than their large-scale counterparts in the Islamic countries. This has been particularly relevant for the construction and service sectors, which have large share in the gross domestic product (GDP). The service sector is made up of many small producers for whom the banking sector has not been able to provide sufficient financing. Many of these small producers, who traditionally were able to obtain interest-based credit facilities on the basis of collateral, are now finding it difficult to raise funds for their operations.

9.8.1.3.   Running businesses

Running businesses frequently need short-term capital as well as working capital and ready cash for miscellaneous on-the-spot purchases and sundry expenses. This is the daily reality in the business world. The PLS scheme is not geared to cater to this need. Even if there is complete trust and exchange of information between the bank and the business, it is nearly impossible or prohibitively costly to estimate the contribution of such short-term financing on the return of a given business. Neither is the much used mark-up system suitable in this case. It looks unlikely to be able to arrive at general rules to cover all the different situations.

Added to this is the delay involved in authorising emergency loans. Often the clients need to have quick access to fresh funds for the immediate needs to prevent possible delays in the project's implementation schedule. According to the set regulations, it is not possible to bridge-finance such requirements and any grant of financial assistance must be made on the basis of the project's appraisal to determine type and terms and conditions of the scheme of financing.

9.8.1.4.   Government Borrowing

In all countries the Government accounts for a major component of the demand for credit – both short-term and long-term. Unlike business loans these borrowings are not always for investment purposes, nor for investment in productive enterprises. Even when invested in productive enterprises they are generally of a longer-term type and of low yield.

Continued borrowing on a fixed rate basis by the Government would inevitably index bank charges to this rate than to the actual profits of borrowing entities.

9.8.2.   Legislation

Existing banking laws do not permit banks to engage directly in business enterprises using depositors' funds. But this is the basic asset acquiring method of Islamic banks. Therefore new legislation and/ or government authorisation are necessary to establish such banks. In Iran a comprehensive legislation was passed to establish Islamic banks. In Pakistan the Central Bank was authorised to take the necessary steps. In other countries either the banks found work-around ways of using existing regulations or were given special accommodation. In all cases government intervention or active support was necessary to establish Islamic banks working under the PLS scheme.

In spite of this, there is still need for further auxiliary legislation in order to fully realise the goals of Islamic banking.

Iran and Pakistan are countries committed to ridding their economies of *riba* and have made immense strides in towards achieving it. Yet there are many legal difficulties still to be solved as has been seen above. In other Muslim countries the authorities actively or passively participate in the establishment of Islamic banks on account of their religious persuasion. Such is not the case in non-Muslim countries. Here establishing Islamic banks involves conformation to the existing laws of the concerned country which generally are not conducive to PLS type of financing in the banking sector.

9.8.3.   Re-training of staff

As one can easily expect, the bank staff will have to acquire many new skills and learn new procedures to operate the Islamic banking system. This is a time consuming process, which is aggravated by two other factors. One, the sheer number of persons that need to be re-trained and, two, the additional staff that need to be recruited and trained to carry out the increased work.

Principles are still to be laid down and techniques and procedures evolved to carry them out. It is only after the satisfactory achievement of these that proper training can begin. This delay and the resulting confusion appear to be among the main reasons for the banks to stick to modes of financing that are close to the familiar interest-based modes.

9.8.4.   Other Limitations

Among the other disincentives from the borrower's point of view are the need to disclose his accounts to the bank if he were to borrow on the PLS basis and the fear that eventually the tax authorities will become wise to the extent of his business and the profits. Several writers have lashed out at the lack of business ethics among the business community, but that is a fact of life at least for the foreseeable future. There is a paucity of survey or case studies of clients to see their reaction to current modes of financing. As such the bankers are not aware of further disincentives that might be there.

9.8.5.   Accounts

When a business is financed under the PLS scheme it is necessary that the actual profit/ loss made using that money be calculated. Though no satisfactory methods have yet been devised, the first requirement for any such activity is to have the necessary accounts. On the borrowers' side there are two difficulties:

- Many small-time businessmen do not keep any accounts, leave alone proper accounts. The time and money costs will cut into his profits. Larger businesses do not like to disclose their real accounts to anybody.
- On the banks' side the effort and expense involved in checking the accounts of many small accounts is prohibitive and will again cut into their own share of the profits.

Thus both sides would prefer to avoid having to calculate the actually realised profit/ loss.

9.8.6. Excess liquidity

Presence of excess liquidity is reported in nearly all Islamic banks. This is not due to reduced demand for credit but due to the inability of the banks to find clients willing to be funded under the new modes of financing. Some of these difficulties are mentioned above under the head 'Financing'. Here the situation is that there is money available on the one hand and there is need for it on the other but the new rules stand in the way of bringing them together. This is a very strange situation – especially in the developing Muslim countries where money is at a premium even for ordinary economic activities, leave alone development efforts. Removal of riba was expected to ease such difficulties, not to aggravate the already existing ones.

9.8.7. Islamic banking in non-Muslim countries

The modern commercial banking system in nearly all countries of the world is mainly evolved from and modelled on the practices in Europe, especially that in the United Kingdom. The philosophical roots of this system revolve around the basic principles of capital certainty for depositors and certainty as to the rate of return on deposits. In order to enforce these principles for the sake of the depositors and to ensure the smooth functioning of the banking system Central Banks have been vested with powers of supervision and control. All banks have to submit to the Central Bank rules. Islamic banks which wish to operate in non-Muslim countries have some difficulties in complying with these rules.

9.8.8. Certainty of capital and return

While the conventional banks guarantee the capital and rate of return, the Islamic banking system, working on the principle of PLS, cannot, by definition, guarantee any fixed rate of return on deposits. Many Islamic banks do not guarantee the capital either, because if there is a loss it has to be deducted from the capital. Thus the basic difference lies in the very roots of the two systems. Consequently countries working under conventional laws are unable to grant permission to institutions which wish to operate under the PLS scheme to function as commercial banks.

9.8.9. Supervision and control

One other major concern is the Central Bank supervision and control. This mainly relates to liquidity requirements and adequacy of capital. These in turn depend on an assessment of the value of assets of the Islamic banks.

It is evident then that even if there is a desire to accommodate the Islamic system, the new procedures that need be developed and the modifications that need be made to existing procedures are so large that the chances of such accommodation in a cautious sector such as banking is very remote indeed. Any relaxation of strict supervision is precluded because should an Islamic bank fail it would undermine the confidence in the whole financial system, with which it is inevitably identified.

9.9. Core Banking System – Islamic Banking

While Islamic Banking, as a practice, is still evolving, there is another dimension to it. For want of clear guidelines, concepts and logic no core banking system product vendor has ventured into developing a software product completely catering to the Islamic Banking needs. (Most of the product vendors claim that they have a module for Islamic banking, but no-one is sure how much it covers). Needless to say, all these mean, in the days to come, even application software meant for banks need to reckon the Islamic Code.

9.10. Chapter Summary

People have needs – food, clothes, houses, machinery, services; the list is endless. Entrepreneurs perceive these needs and develop ways and means of catering to them. They advertise their products and services, people's expectations are raised and people become customers of the entrepreneur. If the customers' needs are fulfilled according to their expectations they continue to patronise the entrepreneur and his enterprise flourishes. Otherwise his enterprise fails and people take to other entrepreneurs.

Banks too are enterprises; they cater to peoples' needs connected with money – safe-keeping, acquiring capital, transferring funds etc. The fact that they existed for centuries and continue to exist and prosper is proof that their methods are good and they fulfil the customers' needs and expectations. Conventional commercial banking system as it operates today is accepted in all countries except the Islamic world where it is received with some reservation. The reservation is on account of the fact that the banking operations involve dealing in interest which is prohibited in Islam. Conventional banks have ignored this concern on the part of their Muslim clientele. Muslims patronised the conventional banks out of necessity and, when another entrepreneur – the Islamic banker – offered to address their concern many Muslims turned to him. The question is: has the new entrepreneur successfully met their concerns, needs and expectations? If not he may have to put up his shutters!

Broadly speaking, banks have three types of different customers: depositors, borrowers and seekers of bank's other services such as money transfer. Since services do not generally involve dealing in interest Muslims have no problem transacting such businesses with conventional banks; neither do Islamic banks experience any problems in providing these services. Among the depositors there are current account holders who too, similarly, have no problems. It is the savings account holders and the borrowers who have reservations in dealing with the conventional banks. In the following paragraphs discuss how well the Islamic banks have succeeded in addressing their customers' special concern.

With only minor changes in their practices, Islamic banks can get rid of all their cumbersome, burdensome and sometimes doubtful forms of financing and offer a clean and efficient interest-free banking. All the necessary ingredients are already there. The modified system will make use of only two forms of financing – loans with a service charge and *Mudaraba* participatory financing – both of which are fully accepted by all Muslim writers on the subject.

Such a system will offer an effective banking system where Islamic banking is obligatory and a powerful alternative to conventional banking where both co-exist. Additionally, such a system will have no problem in obtaining authorisation to operate in non-Muslim countries.

Participatory financing is a unique feature of Islamic banking, and can offer responsible financing to socially and economically relevant development projects. This is an additional service Islamic banks offer over and above the traditional services provided by conventional commercial banks.

*****

Chapter 10. Manual Banking vs. Automated

The present day banking has turned as "Click Banking" from "Brick Banking". During manual banking days bankers used to struggle with the routine Day Book, General Ledger, Balance Sheet, Tallying individual ledgers with General Ledger, Interest Applications on loans and deposits, etc. Every half year closing used to be a grand mela for them. This has consumed lot of efforts of human resources. The time allotted by them for business development was very less. At times people used to spend the whole night for finding out a difference of ₹0.10. If allowed they could have put it from their pocket rather than spending the midnight oil.

Now all these mundane and routine accounting process and tallying the ledgers are taken care by the systems and people's time is available for the core/ main business of the bank. This is reflected in per employee business of the banks.

After the advent of Core Banking Systems, there are no bankers available in banks – in fact they don't need. All the employees have turned out to be Relationship Managers, Marketing Staff and at times computer operators. In a lighter way – if the present employees are asked "How to calculate interest on pre-closure of Fixed Deposit" they would reply "Press F3". Earlier banking industry itself used to be called as Service Industry – servicing to the clients. Now everything is product and hence banking industry do not have clients, but only have customers.

Also on account of Core Banking System the "Branch Banking" has manifested into "Bank Banking".

At the same time, the processes used in manual systems were defined and being in use for centuries. Due to the advent of Core Banking System the processes have to be re-engineered – giving a different dimension to frauds – i.e. e-fraud or IT-frauds. The frauds in banking industry used to be called as "White collar fraud", but now it is all the more applicable, sitting in one place and attacking the entire globe.

In a way the security threats are multi-dimensional and hence the protection forces also should be well-equipped towards the same.

On the other hand, earlier banks used to have kilos of papers of accounts in ledgers. Now the accounts, the transactions, etc., are wealth of Data for the banks. They could very well be analysed and used to customize the products to the specific needs of that particular zone or area.

This chapter is primarily aimed to stress that the focus of the entire banking industry and its security has drastically changed and continue to change.

*****

Chapter 11. Channels of Banking

On account of technological advancement the channels of banking have multifold. The major ones, based on the usage-wise are – Branches, ATMs, Internet and Mobile.

11.1.   Evolution of banking channels

Around half a century of banking changes have given customers more flexibility and better service, while leaving most banks with an evolved — rather than crafted — set of delivery channels and supporting organisations. Meanwhile, emerging communication capabilities have had profound leveraging impacts on the value of these channels:

- Originally deployed to give customers the convenience of doing their banking closer to home or work, bank branches typically provide the full suite of banking services to **any** customer at **any** location by connecting to centralised account information via networks – i.e. Core Banking System.
- The capabilities of ATMs, initially introduced as standalone devices for cash dispensing, expanded dramatically as ATM network, switch and connectivity enabled real-time access to account information. A survey indicates that approximately 65% of all banking customers regularly bank through ATMs.
- Call center - the model of a single, dedicated service center for all telephone requests benefited from emerging nationwide toll-free telephone services in the mid-80s and quickly spread to other industries, including banking.
- The value of personal computers, initially envisioned as standalone devices for personal productivity, exploded as they became access points to the Internet — enabling, among many other things, Internet Banking. Current studies estimate that more than 25% of the households now use the Internet for banking.
- With each new distribution channel, banks have enhanced the ability to deliver customer service. With the right connectivity behind these channels, their value — both to the bank and to its customers — has been amplified.

- As banking customers choose to interact with their banks over a variety of channels, however, it becomes increasingly important for banks to provide a consistent customer experience across all channels.
- While it was originally expected that banks could reduce costs by investing in alternate channels (by migrating transactions from branches to lower-cost channels), most customers actually responded to new banking options by increasing bank interactions— resulting in higher overall costs for banks.
- Additionally, customers are expecting more in terms of breadth of services, speed of execution and consistency across all modes of interaction with their banks. In a 2001 study, 80% of the respondents felt that they should be able to resolve online banking problems through any channel — phone, branch, e-mail or instant messaging.

One biggest challenge for the banks on account for these kinds of tech-savvy channels is **Security**. How much ever security features are added there are people who are well versed in e-frauds and break all these security features. At the same time, to survive in the challenging market, they cannot say **No** to these channels of banking. A war between these go on parallel.

11.2. Branches

In spite of all the convenience of ATM, Internet Banking, etc., still there are customers who would like to do their transaction within the bank premises. They would like to have face to face discussions. There are some banks who charge some fees, if cash is withdrawn within the premises, which can be done through ATM. This is primarily to encourage customers to use the cost effective channels. In western countries there are some virtual banks, which do not have any physical branches at all. Every transaction is done virtually through ATMs, Call Centres, Mobile and Internet.

11.3.   ATMs

This channel has been discussed earlier in other sections. The primary convenience is round the clock access to the account. Here also the security becomes a threat for the banks.

11.4.   Easy Deposits

A deposit machine, accepts cash, and counts the notes, gives access for depositing cash in the account or any other customer's account in the same bank. Non customers can use this channel to pay their utility bills, Mobiles Top ups, etc.

11.5.   Call Centers

All the banking requirements, clarifications, complaints, etc., can be had through the 24 x 7 call centers, which every bank has.

11.6.   Internet Banking

This service is provided through the Internet. Customers can perform financial services and access their accounts from anywhere in the world by logging on to bank's web-site. Online banking is a term used for performing transactions, payments etc., over the Internet. Here also the security is the main concern.

11.7.   Mobile Banking

This channel allows the customers to avail various information and services on the mobile handset and is divided into alert facility, which keeps the customers updated on transaction in the account and request facility. Most of the services available through Internet Banking is also available in Mobile banking. Basically a mobile with Internet connectivity is the requirement.

11.8. Relationship Manager

Relationship Managers, mostly for private banking or business banking, often visiting customers at their homes or businesses and serve the banking needs of the customers at their doorsteps.

11.9. Phone Banking

Telephone banking is a service which allows its customers to perform transactions over the telephone with automated attendant or when requested with telephone operator – this works through IVR – Interactive Voice Recording.

11.10. Video Banking

Video banking is a term used for performing banking transactions or professional banking consultations via a remote video and audio connection. Video banking can be performed via purpose built banking transaction machines (similar to an Automated teller machine), or via a video conference enabled bank branch.

11.11. Costs for Different Channels

The below table compares the cost per transaction through different channels of banking. While the cost may vary between different countries, this gives an idea of difference in cost between different channels. Also some survey results about the usage of different channels of banking in India are illustrated.

Table 4 – Different Banking Channels - Cost comparison

Channel	Cost per txn ₹
Branches	50.00
ATMs	15.00
Net Banking	4.00
Phone Banking	2.00
Mobile Banking	3.00

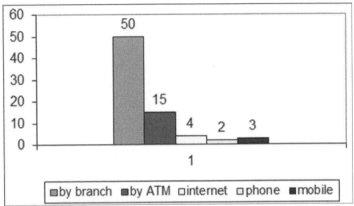

Figure 17 – Different Banking Channels – Cost comparison

11.12. Chapter Summary

The days of branch banking are gone – or at least going. Different channels of banking are taking over the conventional branch channel. On account of technological advancement on a daily basis we can very well expect that this list will never be complete. The cost per transaction also has reduced drastically through these different channels.

- ATMs
- Easy Deposits
- Call Centers
- Internet and Mobile Banking
- Phone Banking
- Relationship Manager

*****

Chapter 12. How to Read a Bank Balance Sheet

When thought of Financial Statements, Banks do prepare Profit & Loss Accounts (P&L) and Balance Sheet (BS) only. Obviously unlike other manufacturing companies, they will not Manufacturing Account and Trading Account. The Manufacturing companies do also prepare Cash and Funds Flow statements, which are not relevant to Banks. The P&L is also called Income & Expenditure statement or Receipts & Payments Statement and BS is also referred to as Sources and Use of funds or Net Worth statement.

The fundamental objective of these financial statements is to reveal and assess the Profitability, Solvency and Liquidity of the Banks.

12.1. Introduction

"Cash Is King?" Sure, all of us have heard the cliché. But what does this really mean? Publicly traded banks are designed to make money. The conventional way of scoring this pursuit is by looking at the bank's ability to grow various flavours of earnings – operating earnings, pretax earnings, net income and earnings per share are all common measures. However, this is not the only way to determine if there is real value in a bank's stock. A bank's real earnings are the earnings that make it from the Consolidated Statement of Earnings to the Balance Sheet as a liquid asset. The second is to look at where tangible shareholder value comes from – returns on invested capital generated by the bank's operations. If a bank has excess liquid assets that it does not need, it can deploy those assets in two ways to benefit shareholders – dividends and stock buybacks.

Knowing what is on the balance sheet is crucial to understanding whether or not the bank, in which the investment is made, is capable of generating real value for shareholders.

12.2. Companies' BS and Banks' BS – a comparison

A company's Balance Sheet – high level – will look like:

Liabilities		Assets	
Capital		Current	
Reserves & Surplus		Fixed	
Current		Investments	
Term		Others	
Total (TL)		Total (TA)	
Net Worth (NW) = Capital + Reserves & Surplus			

A Bank's Balance Sheet – high level – will look like:

Liabilities		Assets	
Capital		Cash & Balance with other banks	
Reserves & Surplus		Money at call & Short Notice	
Deposits		Investments	
Borrowings		Advances	
Other Liabilities & Provisions		Fixed Assets	
		Other Assets	
Total (TL)		Total (TA)	
Contingent Liabilities		Contingent Assets	
Grand Total		Grand Total	
Net Worth (NW) = Capital + Reserves & Surplus			

Further the next level details of each of items would be:

Liabilities

- Net worth
  - Capital – owners funds – Tier I, II and III
  - Reserves & Surplus – Accumulated profits
- Deposits
  - Term/ Demand

- Public/ banks/ others
  - Domestic/ foreign currency
- Borrowings
  - Refinance
  - Other Banks
  - Market
  - Others
- Other liabilities & provisions

Assets

- Cash – both domestic and foreign currency
- Balance with other banks – balance with Central or any other bank
- Money at call and short notice
- Investments – bonds, shares, securities, etc.
- Advances – retail and corporate
- Fixed Assets
- Other Assets

Contingent Liabilities – also called as Off-balance sheet items (as the very names suggest they are not liabilities at present. However, they may turn out to be a liability for the bank in future on account of some other event happening. For instance, banks issue guarantee on behalf of their customers. In a future date, if the customer fails to meet his obligation, banks need to pay the guaranteed amount. Hence this is a contingent liability – an amount that may turn out to be a liability, if the customer fails to meet his obligation. There is nothing like Contingent Asset. However, since we have some Contingent Liability and since the Liabilities and Assets of Balance Sheet have to tally, exactly the same amount is treated as Contingent asset and shown in the balance sheet. These are also called as Non-fund based exposures – since no funds move out of the banks as at present. Examples of contingent liabilities are:

- Bank Guarantees
- LCs
- Derivatives

Profit & Loss Account

- Cash Income
- Cash Expenses
- Net Cash Income = Cash income – Cash Expenses
- Inventory Change
- Depreciation & Capital Adjustments
- Net Income = Net cash income minus inventory change minus depreciation

Major segmentation of Income to be observed and compared to the industry standard is:

Income	
Interest on loans	%
Investments	%
Interest on balance with RBI and other banks	%
Other Income	%
Segment Revenue	
Treasury	%
Corporate Banking	%
Retail Banking	%
Others	%

The areas to be observed and compared with industry standard under **Lending** are:

Lending	
Corporate	%
Retail	%
NPA Gross	%
NPA – net	%
Basel related disclosures	
Tier I, II, III capital – minimum required vs. actuals.	%
Quantitative Disclosures	
Credit Risk Disclosures	
Market Risk Disclosures	
Operational Risk Disclosures	

12.3.   Points to Observe

First of all, the balance sheet is an average balance for the line item, rather than the balance at the end of the period. Average balances provide a better analytical framework to help understand the bank's financial performance. It has to be noted that for each average balance sheet item there is a corresponding interest-related income, or expense item, and the average yield for the time period. It also demonstrates the impact a flattening yield curve can have on a bank's net interest income.

The best place to start is with the net interest income line item. The bank experienced lower net interest income even though it had grown average balances.

Changes in the general level of interest rates may affect the volume of certain types of banking activities that generate fee-related income. For example, the volume of residential mortgage loan originations typically declines as interest rates rise, resulting in lower originating fees. In contrast, mortgage servicing pools often face slower prepayments when rates are rising, since borrowers are less likely to refinance. As a result, fee income and associated economic value arising from mortgage servicing-related businesses may increase or remain stable in periods of moderately rising interest rates. While analysing a bank it should also be considered how interest rate risk may act jointly with other risks facing the bank. For example, in a rising rate environment, loan customers may not be able to meet interest payments because of the increase in the size of the payment or a reduction in earnings. The result will be a higher level of problem loans. An increase in interest rates exposes a bank with a significant concentration in adjustable rate loans to credit risk. For a bank that is predominately funded with short-term liabilities, a rise in rates may decrease net interest income at the same time credit quality problems are on the increase. Credit Risk is most simply defined as the potential that a bank borrower or counterparty will fail to meet its obligations in accordance with agreed terms. When this happens, the bank will experience a loss of some or all of the credit it provided to its customer. To absorb these losses, banks maintain an allowance for loan and lease losses.

In essence, this allowance can be viewed as a pool of capital specifically set aside to absorb estimated loan losses. This allowance should be maintained at a level that is adequate to absorb the estimated amount of probable losses in the institution's loan portfolio.

Actual losses are written off from the balance sheet account 'allowance' for loan and lease losses. The allowance for loan and lease losses is replenished through the income statement line item 'provision' for loan losses, which is treated as an expense.

12.4.   Qualitative analysis of Bank Balance Sheet

An analysis of a Bank's balance sheet should not only be quantitative but also should be qualitative. Some of the important areas in this regard would be:

*   All expenses or provisions or advances or loans etc. which are accrued and payable within 12 months are current liabilities.
*   When a company makes investments in unconnected avenues such as shares, securities, associate concerns are to be treated as non-current assets.
*   The slow moving and absolute inventories
*   Comparison of minimum three years balance sheet would be

meaningful

- It is a mixture of facts, opinions and conventions – the annexures/ Notes to the balance sheet is more vital than the figures.
- While opinions are of the company's management, the conventions are practiced by the finance managers of the company.
- Depreciation method may be changed to boost profit
- It may be silent on key personnel and staff turnover
- Marginal changes in the classification of certain items would lead to different results.

12.5.   Chapter Summary

A bank's balance sheet should reveal – to understand the hidden details is the very purpose of analysing the balance sheet. The reader should understand the following major items:

- Management competence
- Investment decision
- Resorting to window dressing
- The key personnel of the company
- The structure of the organisation
- The authority and decision making – decentralised vs. centralized
- The state of industrial relations
- Financial systems and procedures
- Management control - planning, budgeting, forecasting
- Status of the technology - Capacity utilisation
- Position in the market, competitions, etc.
- For listed banks share prices, EPS, book value, dividend record, public response, etc.

*****

Chapter 13. Banking Landscape

The facet of the entire banking operation has undergone a drastic revolution – thanks to Western Banks and Core Banking Systems. It is primarily classified into; Front Office, Mid Office and Back Office functions.

13.1.   Emerging Economic Scene

The banking system is the lifeline of the economy. The changes in the economy get mirrored in the performance of the banking industry.

The ability of the banking system in its present structure to make available investible resources to the potential investors in the forms and tenors that will be required by them in the coming years, that is, as equity, long term debt and medium and short-term debt would be critical to the achievement of plan objectives. The gap in demand and supply of resources in different segments of the financial markets has to be met and for this, smooth flow of funds between various types of financial institutions and instruments would need to be facilitated. Financing of infrastructure projects is a specialised activity and would continue to be of critical importance in the future. After all, a sound and efficient infrastructure is a sine qua non for sustainable economic development.

13.2.   Banking Operations – Different Perspective

Wherever direct interaction with the customer is involved those operations can be considered as Front office. Mid-office generally validates the front office functions like approval, etc. Back Office functions take care of day-end operations, report generation, routine back-up, etc. There is one more division as support – admin jobs, testing, purchase, etc., normally non-banking related operations. The below diagram gives an overview of various front, mid, back office and support functions.

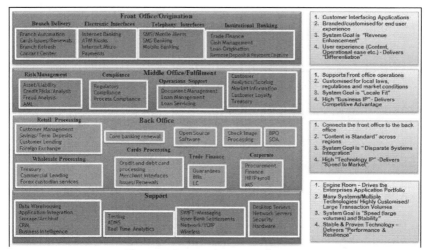

Figure 18 – Banking Landscape

Banking is not just accepting deposits and lending. There are many more functions like Treasury Management, Risk Management, Customer Relationship Management, etc. The author had interacted with many officials of various banks, in different countries. All of them, both developing and developed, unanimously were of same relaxed opinion that once Core Banking System is implemented for the whole of the bank then the automation is complete. But the author scared them by saying that it is only the beginning and there is lot more to act upon. To stress this point the below diagram illustrates the operations around Core Banking:

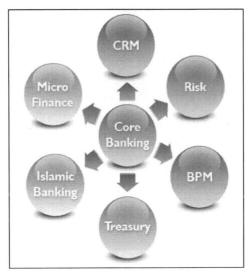

Figure 19 – Around Core Banking

While most of these areas are out of scope of this book; this would give an idea that banking encompasses much more than what we perceive. However, the areas like Islamic Banking and CRM are discussed in other chapters to provide completeness and to make the readers to get an idea of the current trends in the Retail Banking segment. This chapter was aimed at to have a wholesome view of different domains of the Banking industry.

13.3. Dependency on Technology

It is a known factor that the Banking system is globally competitive. To survive in this market, the players will have to be financially strong and operationally efficient. Capital would be a key factor in building a successful institution. The banking system will improve competitiveness through a process of consolidation, either through mergers and acquisitions or through strategic alliances.

Technology would be the key to the competitiveness of banking system. Indian players will keep pace with global leaders in the use of banking technology. In such a scenario, on-line accessibility will be available to the customers from any part of the globe; 'Anywhere' and 'Anytime' banking will be realised truly and fully. At the same time 'brick and mortar' banking will co-exist with 'click' banking to cater to the specific needs of different customers.

Banking system is playing a crucial role in the socio-economic development of the country. The system will continue to be sensitive to the growth and development needs of all the segments of the society.

The banking system that will evolve will be transparent in its dealings and adopt global best practices in accounting and disclosures driven by the motto of value enhancement for all stakeholders.

The banking industry in developing countries like India is moving gradually from a regulated environment to a deregulated market. The market developments kindled by liberalisation and globalisation have resulted in changes in the intermediation role of banks. The pace of transformation has been more significant in recent times with technology acting as a catalyst. While the banking system has done fairly well in adjusting to the new market dynamics, greater challenges lie ahead. Financial sector would be opened up for greater international competition under World Trade Organisation. Banks will have to gear up to meet stringent prudential capital adequacy norms under Basel II (Basel III is already drafted and being adopted in phases). In addition to WTO and Basel II, the Free Trade Agreements (FTAs) such as with Singapore, may have an impact on the shape of the banking industry. Banks will also have to cope with challenges posed by technological innovations in banking. Banks need to prepare for the changes.

13.4. Future Landscape of Banking

Liberalisation and de-regulation processes, in some of the developing countries like India, have made a sea change in the banking system. From a totally regulated environment, the system is moving gradually into a market driven competitive system. The move towards global benchmarks has been, by and large, calibrated and regulator driven. The pace of changes gained momentum in the last decade. Globalisation would gain greater speed in the coming years particularly on account of expected opening up of financial services under WTO. Four trends change the banking industry world over, viz.:

- Consolidation of players through mergers and acquisitions
- Globalisation of operations
- Development of new technology and
- Universalisation of banking

With technology acting as a catalyst, great changes can be expected in the banking scene in the coming years.

The traditional banking functions would give way to a system geared to meet all the financial needs of the customer. The emergence of highly varied financial products, which are tailored to meet specific needs of the customers in the retail as well as corporate segments, can be visualised. The advent of new technologies could see the emergence of new financial players doing financial intermediation. The conventional definition of banking is undergoing complete vicissitudes.

The competitive environment in the banking sector is likely to result in individual players working out differentiated strategies based on their strengths and market niches. For example, some players might emerge as specialists in mortgage products, credit cards etc., whereas some may choose to concentrate on particular segments of business system, while outsourcing all other functions. Some other banks may concentrate on industrial segments or high net worth individuals by providing specially tailored services beyond traditional banking offerings to satisfy the needs of customers they understand better than a more generalist competitor.

Retail lending will receive greater focus. Banks would compete with one another to provide full range of financial services to this segment. Banks would use multiple delivery channels to suit the requirements and tastes of customers. While some customers might value relationship banking (conventional branch banking), others might prefer convenience banking (e-banking).

In the midst of all the advancements, one of the concerns is quality of bank lending. Most significant challenge before banks is the maintenance of rigorous credit standards, especially in an environment of increased competition for new and existing clients. **Experience has shown us that the worst loans are often made in the best of times.**

Structure and ownership pattern would undergo changes. There would be greater presence of international players in any developing country's banking system. Mergers and acquisitions would gather momentum as managements will strive to meet the expectations of stakeholders.

Corporate governance in banks and financial institutions would assume greater importance in the coming years and this will be reflected in the composition of the Boards of Banks.

13.5.   Product Innovation and Process Re-Engineering

With increased competition in the banking Industry, the net interest margin of banks has come down over the last one decade. Liberalisation with Globalisation will see the spreads narrowing further as in the case of banks operating in developed countries. Banks will look for fee-based income to fill the gap in interest income. Product innovations and process re-engineering will be the order of the day. The changes will be motivated by the desire to meet the customer requirements and to reduce the cost and improve the efficiency of service. All banks will therefore go for rejuvenating their costing and pricing to segregate profitable and non-profitable business. The new paradigm in the coming years will be **cost = revenue - profit**.

As banks strive to provide value added services to customers, the market will see the emergence of strong investment and merchant banking entities. Product innovation and creating brand equity for specialised products will decide the market share and volumes. New products on the liabilities side such as Forex linked deposits; investment-linked deposits, etc. are likely to be introduced, as investors with varied risk profiles will look for better yields. There will be more and more of tie-ups between banks, corporate clients and their retail outlets to share a common platform to shore up revenue through increased volumes.

Banks will increasingly act as risk managers to corporate and other entities by offering a variety of risk management products like options, swaps and other aspects of financial management in a multi-currency scenario. Banks will play an active role in the development of derivative products and will offer a variety of hedge products to the corporate sector and other investors. For example, Derivatives in emerging futures market for commodities would be an area offering opportunities for banks. As the integration of markets takes place internationally, sophistication in trading and specialised exchanges for commodities will expand. As these changes take place, banking will play a major role in providing financial support to such exchanges, facilitating settlement systems and enabling wider participation.

13.6. Chapter Summary

On account of technological advancement, globalisation, liberalisation, etc., the banking industry in developing countries is undergoing a manifestation.

- Banks will have to adopt global standards in capital adequacy, income recognition and provisioning norms.
- Risk management setup in Banks will need to be strengthened.
- Benchmark standards could be evolved.
- Payment and settlement system will have to be strengthened to ensure transfer of funds on real time basis eliminating risks associated with transactions and settlement process.
- Regulatory set-up will have to be strengthened, in line with the requirements of a market-led integrated financial system
- Banks will have to adopt best global practices, systems and procedures.
- Banks may have to evaluate on an ongoing basis, internally, the need to effect structural changes in the organisation. This will include capital restructuring through mergers/ acquisitions and other measures in the best business interests.
- There should be constant and continual upgradation of technology in the Banks, benefiting both the customer and the bank. Banks may enter into partnership among themselves for reaping maximum

benefits, through consultations and coordination with reputed IT companies.

- The skills of bank staff should be upgraded continuously through training. In this regard, the banks may have to relook at the existing training modules and effect necessary changes, wherever required. Seminars and conferences on all relevant and emerging issues should be encouraged.

- Banks will have to set up Research and Market Intelligence units within the organisation, so as to remain innovative, to ensure customer satisfaction and to keep abreast of market developments. Banks will have to interact constantly with the industry bodies, trade associations, farming community, academic/ research institutions and initiate studies, pilot projects, etc. for evolving better financial models.

*****

Chapter 14. CRM and Bank Marketing

Today, many businesses including banks realise the importance of Customer Relationship Management (CRM) and its potential to help them acquire new customers, retain existing ones and maximize their lifetime value. At this point, close relationship with customers will require a strong coordination between IT and marketing departments to provide a long-term retention of selected customers. The advent of Call Centers for banks is mainly the first step towards customer relationship manager and marketing. CRM is completely depending on technology concepts like Data Warehouse, Data Mining, Analytics, etc.

This chapter aims at providing an overview of CRM in banks and tries to stress on marketing in banks to survive in the competitive market. At the same time care is taken not to divert the contents of this chapter as more technical.

14.1   Customer Relationship Management in Banks

CRM is a sound business strategy to identify the bank's most profitable customers and prospects, and devote time and attention to expanding account relationships with those customers through individualised marketing, reprising, discretionary decision making, and customised service-all delivered through the various sales channels that the bank uses.

In literature, many definitions were given to describe CRM. The main difference among these definitions is technological and relationship aspects of CRM. Some schools from marketing background emphasize technological side of CRM while the others consider IT perspective of CRM. From marketing aspect, CRM is defined as "a combination of business process and technology that seeks to understand a company's customers from the perspective of who they are, what they do, and what they are like". Technological definition of CRM was given as "the market place of the future is undergoing a technology-driven metamorphosis". Consequently, IT and marketing departments must work closely to implement CRM efficiently. Meanwhile, implementation of CRM in banking sector focused on the evaluation of the critical satisfaction dimensions and the determination of customer groups with distinctive preferences and expectations in the private bank sector. Specifically the customer relationships of new technology-based firms were interested in total sales activities, both volume-related and non-volume related. They also developed a modification of the standard data envelope analysis (DEA) structure using goal programming concepts that yields both a sales and service measures.

14.1.1. Objectives of CRM in Bank

The idea of CRM is that it helps businesses use technology and human resources gain insight into the behavior of customers and the value of those customers. If it works as hoped, a business can provide better customer service, make call centers more efficient, cross sell products more effectively, help sales staff close deals faster, simplify marketing and sales processes, discover new customers, and increase customer revenues. It doesn't happen by simply buying software and installing it. For CRM to be truly effective an organisation must first decide what kind of customer information it is looking for and it must decide what it intends to do with that information. For example, many banks keep track of customers' life stages in order to market appropriate banking products to them at the right time to fit their needs. Next, the organisation must look into all of the different ways information about customers comes into a business, where and how this data is stored and how it is used. Banks, for instance, may interact with customers in a myriad of different ways including mail campaigns, web-sites, brick-and-mortar branches, call centers, mobile sales force staff and marketing and advertising efforts. In reality all these systems link up each of these points.

14.2. Data Warehouse and Data Mining

As mentioned earlier, the banks are sitting on a wealth of data. Data warehouse, the technology system, is the core of any decision support system and hence of the CRM.

The Analytical Datamart is derived from the Data Warehouse through the following raw data processing: data selection, data extraction, and data verification and rectification.

14.3. Marketing Campaigns

After analysing strategic and analytical CRM the concentration should be equally important on operational aspects.

Bank marketing in general and Customer Relationship Management (CRM) in particular are of vital importance for Indian banks particularly in the current context when banks are facing tough competition from other agencies, both local and foreign, that offer value added services. Competition is confined not only to resource mobilization but also to lending and other revenue generating areas of services offered by banks.

Under the circumstances, it has become essential to develop a close relationship with valued customers and come out with innovative measures to satisfy their needs. Customer expectations for quality services and returns are increasing rapidly and, therefore, quality in future will be the sole determinant of successful banking corporations. It is thus high time that Indian banks organically realize the imperative of proactive Bank Marketing and Customer Relationship Management and take systematic steps in this direction.

14.4. Marketing Approach

Banking industry is essentially a service industry which provides various types of banking and allied services to its clients. Bank customers are such persons and organizations that have surplus or shortage of funds and those who need various types of financial and related services provided by the banking sector. These customers belong to different strata of economy, different geographical locations and different professions and businesses.

Naturally, the need of each individual group of customers is distinct from the needs of other groups. It is, therefore, necessary to identify different homogenous groups and even sub-groups of customers, and then with utmost precision determine their needs, design schemes to suit their exact needs, and deliver them most efficiently.

Banks generally have been working out various services and products at the level of the Head Office and these are traded through their retail outlets (branches) to different customers at the grassroots level. This is the so called "top down" approach. However, bank marketing requires a change in this traditional outlook. It should be "bottom to top" approach with customers at the grassroots level as the focal point for working out various products/ schemes to suit the needs of different homogenous groups of customers. Thus, bank marketing approach, in general, is a group or 'collective' approach.

Customers Relationship Management, on the other hand, is an individualistic approach which concentrates on certain select customers from the homogeneous groups, and develops sustainable relationship with them for adding value to the bank. This may be termed as a 'selective' approach.

Thus, bank marketing concept, whether 'collective' approach or 'selective' approach, is a fundamental recognition of the fact that banks need customer oriented approach. In other words, bank marketing is the design and delivery of customer needed services worked out by keeping in view the corporate objectives of the bank and environmental constraints.

Banking Industry is one of the most important service industries which touch the lives of millions of people. Its service is unique both in social and economic points of view of a nation. Earlier the attitude of banking service was that it was not professional to sell one's services and was unnecessary in the sense that traditional relationships and quality of products were sufficient to carry forward the tasks.

14.5. Chapter Summary

Banks have started to focus on Marketing their products through Customers Relationship Management, Call centres, Analytics of data, marketing campaigns, and all other possible ways. Technology supports these iniatives in all possible ways and much more technological innovations are in the pipeline to help the banks marketing their products.

*****

Chapter 15. Anti-Money Laundering

Generally the term Money-laundering is confused with converting black money into white. Conversion of black money into white is definitely an illegal activity, but not under the Anti Money Laundering laws, but under different laws say Income Tax Act.

Another related term confused with Money Laundering is Hawala. This is also an illegal activity. Any foreign currency is to be converted into domestic currency only through approved banking channels. If otherwise converted it is Hawala. For instance if ABC borrows US$ 1,000 from his friend XYZ and pays his Indian Rupee equivalent, it is hawala. This is also illegal under FERA or FEMA or equivalent laws in other countries. Again this is not money laundering.

Money laundering is the process of concealing the source of money obtained by illicit means. The methods by which money may be laundered are varied and can range in sophistication. Many regulatory and governmental authorities quote estimates each year for the amount of money laundered, either worldwide or within their national economy. In 1996, the International Monetary Fund estimated that two to five percent of the worldwide global economy involved laundered money. However, the Financial Action Task Force on Money Laundering (FATF), an intergovernmental body set up to combat money laundering, stated that "overall it is absolutely impossible to produce a reliable estimate of the amount of money laundered and therefore the FATF does not publish any figures in this regard". Academic commentators have likewise been unable to estimate the volume of money with any degree of assurance.

Regardless of the difficulty in measurement, the amount of money laundered each year is in the billions (US dollars) and poses a significant policy concern for governments. As a result, governments and international bodies have undertaken efforts to deter, prevent and apprehend money launderers. Financial institutions have likewise undertaken efforts to prevent and detect transactions involving dirty money, both as a result of government requirements and to avoid the reputational risk involved.

15.1. Methods

Money laundering often occurs in three steps: first, cash is introduced into the financial system by some means ('placement'); the second involves carrying out complex financial transactions in order to camouflage the illegal source ('layering'); and, the final step entails acquiring wealth generated from the transactions of the illicit funds ('integration'). Some of these steps may be omitted, depending on the circumstances; for example, non-cash proceeds that are already in the financial system would have no need for placement.

Money laundering takes several different forms, although most methods can be categorized into one of a few types. These include "bank methods, smurfing [also known as structuring], currency exchanges, and double-invoicing".

- **Structuring**: Often known as 'smurfing', is a method of placement by which cash is broken into smaller deposits of money, used to defeat suspicion of money laundering and to avoid anti-money laundering reporting requirements. A sub-component of this is to use smaller amounts of cash to purchase bearer instruments, such as money orders, and then ultimately deposit those, again in small amounts.
- **Bulk cash smuggling**: Physically smuggling cash to another jurisdiction, where it will be deposited in a financial institution, such as an offshore bank, with greater bank secrecy or less rigorous money laundering enforcement.
- **Cash-intensive businesses**: A business typically involved in receiving cash will use its accounts to deposit both legitimate and criminally derived cash, claiming all of it as legitimate earnings. Best suited is a service business. As such business has no variable costs, it is hard to detect revenues-costs discrepancies. Examples are parking buildings, strip clubs, tanning beds or a casino.
- **Trade-based laundering**: Under- or over-valuing invoices in order to disguise the movement of money.

- **Shell companies and trusts**: Trusts and shell companies disguise the true owner of money. Trusts and corporate vehicles, depending on the jurisdiction, need not disclose their true, beneficial, owner.
- **Round-tripping**: Money is deposited in a controlled foreign corporation offshore, preferably in a tax haven where minimal records are kept, and then shipped back as a Foreign Direct Investment, exempt from taxation.
- **Bank capture**: Money launderers or criminals buy a controlling interest in a bank, preferably in a jurisdiction with weak money laundering controls, and then move money through the bank without scrutiny.
- **Casinos**: An individual will walk into a casino with cash and buy chips, play for a while and then cash in his or her chips, for which he or she will be issued a check. The money launderer will then be able to deposit the check into his or her bank account, and claim it as gambling winnings.
- **Real estate**: Real estate may be purchased with illegal proceeds, then sold. The proceeds from the sale appear to outsiders to be legitimate income. Alternatively, the price of the property is manipulated; the seller will agree to a contract that under-represents the value of the property, and will receive criminal proceeds to make up the difference.
- **Black salaries**: Companies might have unregistered employees without a written contract who are given cash salaries. Black cash might be used to pay them.
- **Fictional loans**

15.2.   Enforcement

Anti-money laundering (AML) is a term mainly used in the financial and legal industries to describe the legal controls that require financial institutions and other regulated entities to prevent, detect and report money laundering activities. Anti-money laundering guidelines came into prominence globally as a result of the formation of the Financial Action Task Force (FATF) and the promulgation of an international framework of anti-money laundering standards. These standards began to have more relevance in 2000 and 2001 after FATF began a process to publicly identify countries that were deficient in their anti-money laundering laws and international cooperation, a process colloquially known as "name and shame".

An effective AML program requires a jurisdiction to have criminalized money laundering, given the relevant regulators and police the powers and tools to investigate; be able to share information with other countries as appropriate; and require financial institutions to identify their customers, establish risk-based controls, keep records, and report suspicious activities.

15.3. Criminalizing money laundering:

The elements of the crime of money laundering are set forth in the United Nations Convention Against Illicit Traffic in Narcotic Drugs and Psychotropic Substances and Convention against Transnational Organized Crime. It is knowingly engaging in a financial transaction with the proceeds of a crime for the purpose of concealing or disguising the illicit origin of the property.

15.4. The role of financial institutions:

Today, most financial institutions globally, and many non-financial institutions, are required to identify and report transactions of a suspicious nature to the financial intelligence unit in the respective country. For example, a bank must verify a customer's identity and, if necessary, monitor transactions for suspicious activity. This is often termed as KYC – "know your customer". This means, to begin with, knowing the identity of the customers, and further, understanding the kinds of transactions in which the customer is likely to engage. By knowing one's customers, financial institutions will often be able to identify unusual or suspicious behavior, termed anomalies, which may be an indication of money laundering.

Bank employees, such as tellers and customer account representatives, are trained in anti-money laundering and are instructed to report activities that they deem suspicious. Additionally, anti-money laundering software filters customer data, classifies it according to level of suspicion, and inspects it for anomalies. Such anomalies would include any sudden and substantial increase in funds, a large withdrawal, or moving money to a bank secrecy jurisdiction. Smaller transactions that meet certain criteria may also be flagged as suspicious. For example, structuring can lead to flagged transactions. The software will also flag names that have been placed on government "blacklists" and transactions involving countries that are thought to be hostile to the host nation. Once the software has mined data and flagged suspect transactions, it alerts bank management, who must then determine whether to file a report with the government.

15.5. Value of enforcement costs and associated concerns

The financial services industry has become more vocal about the rising costs of antimoney laundering regulation, and the limited benefits that they claim it appears to bring. The Economist magazine has become increasingly vocal in its criticism of such regulation, particularly with reference to countering terrorist financing, referring to it as a "costly failure", although concedes that the rules to combat money laundering are more effective.

However, there is no precise measurement of the costs of regulation balanced against the harms associated with money laundering and given the evaluation problems involved in assessing such an issue, it is unlikely the effectiveness of terror finance and money laundering laws could be determined with any degree of accuracy. Government-linked economists have noted the significant negative effects of money laundering on economic development, including undermining domestic capital formation, depressing growth, and diverting capital away from development.

Data privacy has also been raised as a concern. A European Union working party, for example, has announced a list of 44 recommendations to better harmonize, and if necessary pare back, the money laundering laws of EU member states to comply with fundamental privacy rights. In the United States, groups such as the American Civil Liberties Union have expressed concern that money laundering rules require banks to report on their own customers, essentially conscripting private businesses "into agents of the surveillance state".

In any event, many countries are obligated by various international instruments and standards, such as the United Nations Convention Against Illicit Traffic in Narcotic Drugs and Psychotropic Substances, the Convention against Transnational Organized Crime, and the United Nations Convention against Corruption, and the recommendations of the FATF to enact and enforce money laundering laws in an effort to stop narcotics trafficking, international organised crime, and corruption. Other countries, such as Mexico, which are faced with significant crime problems believe that anti-money laundering controls could help curb the underlying crime issue.

15.6.   Organizations working against money laundering:

Formed in 1989 by the G7 countries, the FATF is an intergovernmental body whose purpose is to develop and promote an international response to combat money laundering. The FATF Secretariat is housed at the headquarters of the OECD in Paris. In October 2001, FATF expanded its mission to include combating the financing of terrorism. FATF is a policy-making body, which brings together legal, financial and law enforcement experts to achieve national legislation and regulatory AML and CFT reforms. Currently, its membership consists of 34 countries and territories and two regional organizations. In addition, FATF works in collaboration with a number of international bodies and organizations. These entities have observer status with FATF, which does not entitle them to vote, but permits full participation in plenary sessions and working groups.

FATF has developed 40 Recommendations on money laundering and 9 Special Recommendations regarding terrorist financing. FATF assesses each member country against these recommendations in published reports. Countries seen as not being sufficiently compliant with such recommendations are subjected to financial sanctions.

FATF's three primary functions with regard to money laundering are:

1. Monitoring members' progress in implementing anti-money laundering measures.
2. Reviewing and reporting on laundering trends, techniques and countermeasures.
3. Promoting the adoption and implementation of FATF anti-money laundering standards globally.

The FATF currently comprises 34 member jurisdictions and 2 regional organisations, representing most major financial centres in all parts of the globe.

The United Nations Office on Drugs and Crime maintains the International Money Laundering Information Network, a website that provides information and software for anti-money laundering data collection and analysis. The World Bank has a website in which it provides policy advice and best practices to governments and the private sector on anti-money laundering issues.

15.7. Laws and enforcement by region

Many jurisdictions adopt a list of specific predicate crimes for money laundering prosecutions, while others criminalize the proceeds of any serious crime.

Afghanistan

The Financial Transactions and Reports Analysis Center of Afghanistan (FinTRACA) was established as a Financial Intelligence Unit (FIU) under the Anti Money Laundering and Proceeds of Crime Law passed by decree late in 2004. The main purpose of this law is to protect the integrity of the Afghan financial system and to gain compliance with international treaties and conventions. The Financial Intelligence Unit is a semi-independent body that is administratively housed within the Central Bank of Afghanistan (Da Afghanistan Bank). The main objective of FinTRACA is to deny the use of the Afghan financial system to those who obtained funds as the result of illegal activity, and to those who would use it to support terrorist activities.

To meet its objectives, the FinTRACA collects and analyzes information from a variety of sources. These sources include entities with legal obligations to submit reports to the FinTRACA when a suspicious activity is detected, as well as reports of cash transactions above a threshold amount specified by regulation. Also, FinTRACA has access to all related Afghan government information and databases. When the analysis of this information supports the supposition of illegal use of the financial system, the FinTRACA works closely with law enforcement to investigate and prosecute the illegal activity. FinTRACA also cooperates internationally in support of its own analyses and investigations and to support the analyses and investigations of foreign counterparts, to the extent allowed by law. Other functions include training of those entities with legal obligations to report information, development of laws and regulations to support national-level AML objectives, and international and regional cooperation in the development of AML typologies and countermeasures.

Australia

AUSTRAC (Australian Transaction Reports and Analysis Centre) is Australia's anti-money laundering and counter-terrorism financing regulator and specialist financial intelligence unit.

The Anti-Money Laundering & Counter Terrorism Financing 2006 (AMLCTF) is the principal legislative instrument, although there are also offence provisions introduced into the Crimes Act 1901 (Cth). Upon its introduction the AMLCTF was to be further amended by a second tranche of reforms to extend inter alia to other commercial contexts such as real estate agents, but those further reforms have since not been effectuated. AUSTRAC works collaboratively with Australian industries and businesses in their compliance with anti-money laundering and counter-terrorism financing legislation. Financial institutions in Australia are required to track significant cash transactions (greater than A$10,000.00 or equivalent in physical cash value) that can be used to finance terrorist activities in and outside Australia's borders and report them to AUSTRAC.

Bangladesh

In Bangladesh, this issue has been dealt with by the Prevention of Money Laundering Act, 2002 (Act No. VII of 2002). In terms of section 2, "Money Laundering means:

A. Properties acquired or earned directly or indirectly through illegal means;
B. Illegal transfer, conversion, concealment of location or assistance in the above act of the properties acquired or earned directly of indirectly through legal or illegal means".

In this Act, 'properties' means movable or immovable properties of any nature and description.

To prevent these Illegal uses of money, the Bangladesh government has introduced the Money Laundering Prevention Act. The Act was last amended in the year 2009 and all the financial institutes are following this act. Till today there are 26 circulars issued by Bangladesh Bank under this act. To prevent money laundering, a banker must do the following:

*   While opening a new account, the account opening form should be duly filled up by all the information of the customer.
*   The KYC has to be properly filled.
*   The Transaction Profile (TP) is mandatory for a client to understand his/ her transactions. If needed, the TP has to be updated at the client's consent.
*   All other necessary papers should be properly collected along with the voter ID card.
*   If any suspicious transaction is noticed, the Branch Anti Money Laundering Compliance Officer (BAMLCO) has to be notified and accordingly the Suspicious Transaction Report (STR) has to be done.
*   The cash department should be aware of the transactions. It has to be noted if suddenly a big amount of money is deposited in any account. Proper documents will be required if any client does this type of transaction.

- Structuring, over/ under invoicing is another way to do money laundering. The foreign exchange department should look into this matter cautiously.
- If in any account there is a transaction exceeding 7.00 lakh in a single day that has to be reported as Cash Transaction Report (CTR).
- All bank officials must go through all the 26 circulars and use them.

Canada

FINTRAC (Financial Transaction and Reports Analysis Centre of Canada) is responsible for investigation of money and terrorist financing cases that are originating from or destined for Canada. The financial intelligence unit was created by the amendment of the Proceeds of Crime (Money Laundering) Act in December 2001 and created the Proceeds of Crime (Money Laundering) and Terrorist Financing Act.

Financial institutions in Canada are required to track large cash transactions (daily total greater than CAD$10,000.00 or equivalent value in other currencies) that can be used to finance terrorist activities in and beyond Canada's borders and report them to FINTRAC.

European Union

The EU directive 2005/60/EC "on the prevention of the use of the financial system for the purpose of money laundering and terrorist financing" tries to prevent such crime by requiring banks, real estate agents and many more companies to investigate and report usage of cash in excess of €15,000. The earlier EU directives 91/308/EEC and 2001/97/EC also relate to money laundering.

India

The Prevention of Money-Laundering Act, 2002 came into effect on 01st July 2005.
Section 12 (1) prescribes the obligations on banks, financial institutions and intermediaries (a) to maintain records detailing the nature and value of transactions which may be prescribed, whether such transactions comprise of a single transaction or a series of transactions integrally

connected to each other, and where such series of transactions take place within a month; (b) to furnish information of transactions referred to in clause (a) to the Director within such time as may be prescribed and t records of the identity of all its clients. Section 12 (2) prescribes that the records referred to in sub-section (1) as mentioned above, must be maintained for ten years after the transactions finished. It is handled by the Indian Income Tax Department.

The provisions of the Act are frequently reviewed and various amendments have been passed from time to time.

The recent activity in money laundering in India is through political parties, corporate companies and the shares market. It is investigated by the Indian Income Tax Department.

Bank accountants must record all the transactions whose amount will be more than ₹. 10 Lakhs. Bank accountants must maintain this records for 10 years. Banks will also make cash transaction reports (CTRs) and Suspicious transaction reports whose amounts are more than ₹. 10 Lakhs within 7 days of doubt. This report will be submitted to enforcement directorate and income tax department.

United Kingdom

Money laundering and terrorist funding legislation in the UK is governed by four Acts of primary legislation:-

- Terrorism Act 2000
- Anti-terrorism, Crime and Security Act 2001
- Proceeds of Crime Act 2002
- Serious Organised Crime and Police Act 2005
- Money Laundering Regulations 2007

Money Laundering Regulations are designed to protect the UK financial system. If a business is covered by these regulations then controls are put in place to prevent it being used for money laundering.

The Proceeds of Crime Act 2002 contains the primary UK anti-money laundering legislation, including provisions requiring businesses within the 'regulated sector' (banking, investment, money transmission, certain professions, etc.) to report to the authorities suspicions of money laundering by customers or others.

Money laundering is widely defined in the UK. In effect any handling or involvement with any proceeds of any crime (or monies or assets representing the proceeds of crime) can be a money laundering offence. An offender's possession of the proceeds of his own crime falls within the UK definition of money laundering. The definition also covers activities which would fall within the traditional definition of money laundering as a process by which proceeds of crime are concealed or disguised so that they may be made to appear to be of legitimate origin.

Unlike certain other jurisdictions (notably the USA and much of Europe), UK money laundering offences are not limited to the proceeds of serious crimes, nor are there any monetary limits, nor is there any necessity for there to be a money laundering design or purpose to an action for it to amount to a money laundering offence. A money laundering offence under UK legislation need not involve money, since the money laundering legislation covers assets of any description. In consequence any person who commits an acquisitive crime (i.e. one from which he obtains some benefit in the form of money or an asset of any description) in the UK will inevitably also commit a money laundering offence under UK legislation.

This applies also to a person who, by criminal conduct, evades a liability (such as a taxation liability) – referred to by lawyers as "obtaining a pecuniary advantage" – as he is deemed thereby to obtain a sum of money equal in value to the liability evaded.

The principal money laundering offences carry a maximum penalty of 14 years imprisonment.

Secondary regulation is provided by the Money Laundering Regulations 2003, which was replaced by the Money Laundering Regulations 2007. They are directly based on the EU directives 91/308/EEC, 2001/97/EC and 2005/60/EC.

One consequence of the Act is that solicitors, accountants, tax advisers and insolvency practitioners who suspect (as a consequence of information received in the course of their work) that their clients (or others) have engaged in tax evasion or other criminal conduct from which a benefit has been obtained, are now required to report their suspicions to the authorities (since these entail suspicions of money laundering). In most circumstances it would be an offence, 'tipping-off', for the reporter to inform the subject of his report that a report has been made. These provisions do not however require disclosure to the authorities of information received by certain professionals in privileged circumstances or where the information is subject to legal professional privilege. Others that are subject to these regulations include financial institutions, credit institutions, estate agents (which includes chartered surveyors), trust and company service providers, high value dealers (who accept cash equivalent to €15,000 or more for goods sold), and casinos.

Professional guidance (which is submitted to and approved by the UK Treasury) is provided by industry groups including the Joint Money Laundering Steering Group, the Law Society. and the Consultative Committee of Accountancy Bodies (CCAB). However there is no obligation on banking institutions to routinely report monetary deposits or transfers above a specified value. Instead reports have to be made of all suspicious deposits or transfers, irrespective of their value.

The reporting obligations include reporting suspicions relating to gains from conduct carried out in other countries which would be criminal if it took place in the UK. Exceptions were later added to exempt certain activities which were legal in the location where they took place, such as bullfighting in Spain.

There are more than 200,000 reports of suspected money laundering submitted annually to the authorities in the UK (there were 240,582 reports in the year ended 30 September 2010 – an increase from the 228,834 reports submitted in the previous year). Most of these reports are submitted by banks and similar financial institutions (there were

186,897 reports from the banking sector in the year ended 30 September 2010).

Although 5,108 different organisations submitted suspicious activity reports to the authorities in the year ended 30 September 2010 just four organisations submitted approximately half of all reports, and the top 20 reporting organisations accounted for three-quarters of all reports.

The offence of failing to report a suspicion of money laundering by another person carries a maximum penalty of 5 years imprisonment.

Bureaux de change

All UK Bureaux de change are registered with Her Majesty's Revenue and Customs which issues a trading licence for each location. Bureaux de change and money transmitters, such as Western Union outlets, in the UK fall within the 'regulated sector' and are required to comply with the Money Laundering Regulations 2007. Checks can be carried out by HMRC on all Money Service Businesses.

United States

The US is the pioneer in AML regulations and most of the other countries follow suit. The approach in the United States to stopping money laundering is usefully broken into two areas: preventive (regulatory) measures and criminal measures.

Preventive

In an attempt to prevent dirty money from entering the US financial system in the first place, the United States Congress passed a series of laws, starting in 1970, collectively known as the Bank Secrecy Act. These laws, contained in sections 5311 through 5332 of Title 31 of the United States Code, require financial institutions, which under the current definition include a broad array of entities, including banks, credit card companies, life insurers, money service businesses and broker-dealers in securities, to report certain transactions to the United States Treasury. Cash transactions in excess of US$10,000 must be reported on a currency transaction report (CTR), identifying the individual making the transaction as well as the source of the cash. The US is one of the few countries in the world to require reporting of all cash transactions over a certain limit, although certain businesses can be exempt from the requirement. Additionally, financial institutions must report transaction on a Suspicious Activity Report (SAR) that they deem 'suspicious', defined as a knowing or suspecting that the funds come from illegal activity or disguise funds from illegal activity, that it is structured to evade BSA requirements or appears to serve no known business or apparent lawful purpose; or that the institution is being used to facilitate criminal activity. Attempts by customers to circumvent the BSA, generally by structuring cash deposits to amounts lower than US$10,000 by breaking them up and depositing them on different days or at different locations also violates the law.

The financial database created by these reports is administered by the U.S.'s Financial Intelligence Unit (FIU), called the Financial Crimes Enforcement Network (FinCEN), which is located in Vienna, Virginia. These reports are made available to US criminal investigators, as well as other FIU's around the globe, and FinCEN will conduct computer assisted analyses of these reports to determine trends and refer investigations.

The BSA requires financial institutions to engage in customer due diligence, which is sometimes known in the parlance as "know your customer". This includes obtaining satisfactory identification to give assurance that the account is in the customer's true name, and having an understanding of the expected nature and source of the money that will flow through the customer's accounts. Other classes of customers, such as those with private banking accounts and those of foreign government officials, are subjected to enhanced due diligence because the law deems that those types of accounts are a higher risk for money laundering. All accounts are subject to ongoing monitoring, in which internal bank software scrutinizes transactions and flags for manual inspection those that fall outside certain parameters. If a manual inspection reveals that the transaction is suspicious, the institution should file a Suspicious Activity Report.

The regulators of the industries involved are responsible to ensure that the financial institutions comply with the BSA. For example, the Federal Reserve and the Office of the Comptroller of the Currency regularly inspect banks, and may impose civil fines or refer matters for criminal prosecution for non-compliance. A number of banks have been fined and prosecuted for failure to comply with the BSA. Most famously, Riggs Bank, in Washington D.C., was prosecuted and functionally driven out of business as a result of its failure to apply proper money laundering controls, particularly as it related to foreign political figures.

In addition to the BSA, the U.S. imposes controls on the movement of currency across its borders, requiring individuals to report the transportation of cash in excess of US$10,000 on a form called Report of International Transportation of Currency or Monetary Instruments (known as a CMIR). Likewise, businesses, such as automobile dealerships, that receive cash in excess of US$10,000 must likewise file a Form 8300 with the Internal Revenue Service, identifying the source of the cash.

On 01st September 2010, the Financial Crimes Enforcement Network issued an advisory on "informal value transfer systems" referencing United States v. Banki.

Criminal sanctions

Money laundering has been criminalized in the United States since the Money Laundering Control Act of 1986. That legislation, contained at section 1956 of Title 18 of the United States Code, prohibits individuals from engaging in a financial transaction with proceeds that were generated from certain specific crimes, known as "specified unlawful activities" (SUAs). Additionally, the law requires that an individual specifically intend in making the transaction to conceal the source, ownership or control of the funds. There is no minimum threshold of money, nor is there the requirement that the transaction succeed in actually disguising the money. Moreover, a "financial transaction" has been broadly defined, and need not involve a financial institution, or even a business. Merely passing money from one person to another, so long as it is done with the intent to disguise the source, ownership, location or control of the money, has been deemed a financial transaction under the law. However, the lone possession of money without either a financial transaction or an intent to conceal is not a crime in the United States.

In addition to money laundering, the law, contained in section 1957 of Title 18 of the United States Code, prohibits spending in excess of US$10,000 derived from an SUA, regardless of whether the individual wishes to disguise it. This carries a lesser penalty than money laundering, and unlike the money laundering statute, requires that the money pass through a financial institution.

According to the records compiled by the United States Sentencing Commission, in 2009, the United States Department of Justice typically convicted a little over 81,000 people; of this, approximately 800 are convicted of money laundering as the primary or most serious charge.

*****

Appendix 1 – Major Islamic Banking Terminologies

Table 5 – Islamic Banking Terms

Bai' al 'inah	Sale and buy-back agreement
Bai' bithaman ajil	Deferred payment sale
Bai' muajjal	Credit sale
Bai Salam	A contract in which advance payment is made for goods to be delivered later on.
Dyan	Debt
Gharar	Speculative Transactions
Haraam	Investing in unlawful business
Hibah	Gift
Ijarah	Lease, rent or wage.
Ijarah thumma al bai'	Hire purchase
Ijarah-wal-iqtina	A contract under which an **Islamic bank** provides equipment, building, or other assets to the client against an agreed rental together with a unilateral undertaking by the bank or the client that at the end of the lease period, the ownership in the asset would be transferred to the lessee.
Madharaba	A financial institution provides all the capital and the other partner, the entrepreneur, provides no capital.
Maysir	Ownership depends on predetermined or uncertain event of future
Mudarabah	Profit Sharing – is a contract, with one party providing 100 percent of the capital and the other party providing its specialist knowledge to invest the capital and manage the investment project. Profits generated are shared between the parties according to a pre-agreed ratio. Compared to Musharaka, in a Mudaraba only the lender of the money has to take losses
Murabahah Muajjal	A contract in which the bank earns a profit margin on the purchase price and allows the buyer to pay the price of the commodity at a future date in a lump sum or in installments

Musawamah	*Musawamah* is the negotiation of a selling price between two parties without reference by the seller to either costs or asking price.
Musharakah	Joint Venture - an agreement between two or more partners, whereby each partner provides funds to be used in a venture
Qard hassan/ Qardul hassan	Good loan/ benevolent loan
Riba	Interest
Salaam	Sale
Sharia	Islamic Law
Sukuk	Islamic bonds
Takaful	Islamic insurance
Usury	Collection or payment of interest
Wadiah	Safekeeping
Wakalah	Power of attorney

*****

Appendix 2 – Glossary

This author has separately written a book titled "Dictionary of Financial Terms", wherein Myriad of Global Financial Terms are demystified. However some of the important terms are explained below:

Table 6 – Some of the banking terms

Co-obligant(s)	In the case of joint loans the second, third, etc., named borrowers, is called co-obligant(s). All of them combinedly called as Joint Borrowers.
Guarantee	Please refer Surety
Negotiable Instrument	Any financial instrument like Cheque, Demand Draft, etc., which are negotiable under Negotiable Instruments Act.
Primary Security	The goods for purchase of which the loan is sanctioned is offered as security to the Bank. For instance, in the case of vehicle loan, the vehicle is hypothecated to the bank and it is the primary security. (Please also refer secondary security).
Secondary Security	In addition to the primary security, if additional security is offered to the lender then it is called as secondary security.
Surety	In addition to the borrower, the lenders take surety/ guarantee from an additional person on whom the banks can fall back if the borrower fails to repay.

*****

Appendix 3 – List of Abbreviations

Table 7 – Expansion of the abbreviations used

#	Abbreviation	Expansion
1.	A or S	Anyone or Survivor(s)
2.	ABSA	Application Supported by Blocked Amount
3.	ACH	Automated Clearing House
4.	ALM	Asset Liability Management
5.	AML	Anti-Money Laundering
6.	AMLCTF	Anti-Money Laundering & Counter Terrorism Financing
7.	ARM	Adjustable Rate Mortgage
8.	ATM	Automated Teller Machines
9.	AUSTRAC	Australian Transaction Reports and Analysis Centre
10.	BACS	Bankers' Automated Clearing System
11.	BAMLCO	Branch Anti Money Laundering Compliance Officer
12.	BC	Business Consultant
13.	BS	Balance Sheet
14.	BSA	Banking Secrecy Act
15.	CCAB	Consultative Committee of Accountancy Bodies
16.	CCC	Cheque and Credit Clearing
17.	CHAPS	Clearing House Automated Payment System
18.	CHIPS	Clearing House for Inter-Bank Payment System
19.	CSP	Customer Service Points
20.	CTF	Combating Terrorist Financing
21.	CTR	Cash Transaction Report
22.	CVV	Card Verification Value
23.	DEA	Data Envelope Analysis
24.	DGS	Deferred Gross Settlement

#	Abbreviation	Expansion
25.	DICGC	Deposit Insurance Corporation & Guarantee Corporation of India
26.	DMS	Decision Making System
27.	DNS	Deferred Net Systems
28.	DP	Drawing Power
29.	DSS	Decision Support System
30.	E or S	Either or Survivor
31.	ECS	Electronic Clearing System
32.	EFT	Electronic Funds Transfer
33.	EFTPoS	Electronic Funds Transfer at the Point of Sale
34.	EMI	Equated Monthly Installments
35.	EoD	End of Day
36.	F or S	Former or Survivor
37.	FCNR	Foreign Currency Non-Resident
38.	FCYCS	Foreign Currency Yen Clearing System
39.	FDIC	Federal Deposit Insurance Corporation
40.	FEMA	Foreign Exchange Monitoring Act
41.	FI	Financial Inclusion
42.	FinCEN	Financial Crimes Enforcement Network
43.	FINTRAC	Financial Transaction and Reports Analysis Centre of Canada
44.	FinTRACA	Financial Transactions and Reports Analysis Center of Afghanistan
45.	FIU	Financial Intelligence Unit
46.	FSA	Financial Supervision Authority
47.	FTA	Free Trade Agreement
48.	GDP	Gross Domestic Product
49.	GPM	Graduated Payment Mortgage
50.	HKD	Hong Kong Dollars
51.	HOE	Home Owner's Equity
52.	HSBC	Hong Kong and Shanghai Banking Corporation
53.	I-T	Income Tax
54.	IPO	Initial Public Offering
55.	IT	Information Technology
56.	LVTS	Large Value Transfer System
57.	LC	Letter(s) of Credit

#	Abbreviation	Expansion
58.	LIBOR	London Interbank offered rate
59.	KYC	Know Your Customer
60.	MIBOR	Mumbai Interbank offered rate
61.	NBFC	Non-Banking Financial Corporation
62.	NGO	Non-Governmental Organisation
63.	NPA	Non-Performing Assets
64.	NRE	Non Resident External
65.	NRI	Non Resident Indian
66.	NRO	Non Resident Ordinary
67.	P & L	Profit & Loss Accounts
68.	PDA	Personal Digital Assistant
69.	PIN	Personnel Identification Number
70.	PLR	Prime Lending Rate
71.	PLS	Profit and Loss Sharing
72.	PoS	Point of Sales
73.	OD	Overdraft
74.	ROI	Rate of Interest
75.	RBI	Reserve Bank of India
76.	RFCD	Resident Foreign Currency Deposits
77.	RFID	Radio Frequency Identification
78.	RTGS	Real Time Gross Settlement
79.	SAR	Suspicious Activity Report
80.	SB	Savings Bank accounts
81.	SBI	State Bank of India
82.	SEPA	Single Euro Payments Area
83.	SHG	Self Help Group(s)
84.	SIBOR	Singapore Interbank offered rate
85.	SPNS	Shared Payment Network System
86.	STP	Straight Through Processing
87.	STR	Suspicious Transaction Report
88.	SUAs	Specified Unlawful Activities
89.	SWIFT	Society for Worldwide Interbank Financial Telecommunication.

#	Abbreviation	Expansion
90.	TARGET	Trans-European Automated Real Time Gross Settlement Express Transfer
91.	TP	Transaction Profile
92.	UK	United Kingdom
93.	USD	U.S. Dollars
94.	USP	Unique Selling Proposition
95.	WTO	World Trade Organisation

*****

Appendix 4 – List of Figures

*****

Appendix 5 – List of Tables

*****

About the Author
http://ramamurthy.jaagruti.co.in

Dr. Ramamurthy is a versatile personality having experience and expertise in various areas of Banking, related IT solutions, Information Security, IT Audit, Vedas, Samskrit and so on.

His thirst for continuous learning does not subside. Even at the age of late fifties, he did research on an unique topic "Information Technology and Samskrit" and obtained Ph.D. - doctorate degreefrom University of Madras. He is into a project of developing a Samskrit based compiler.

It is his passion to spread his knowledge and experience through conducting classes, training programmes and writing books.
He has already published books:

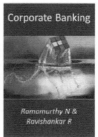

His other books are being published:

Books being penned - Corporate Finance, Banking – GRC, Information Security in Banks, Sri Devee Mahaatmeeyam, Sri Devi Bhagavatam and many more.

Let us all wish him a long and healthy life so that he could continue his services.

*****

5583902R00118

Printed in Great Britain
by Amazon.co.uk, Ltd.,
Marston Gate.